Tales from Shakespeare

CHARLES AND MARY LAMB

Retold by Christopher Williams
Series Editors Hopkins and Jocelyn Potter

Pearson Education Limited
Edinburgh Gate, Harlow,
Essex CM20 2JE, England
and Associated Companies throughout the world.

ISBN: 978-1-4058-6522-7

First published in the Longman Simplified English Series 1933
First published in the Longman Fiction Series 1993
This adaptation first published in 1996
First Penguin Books edition published 1999

5 7 9 10 8 6 4

Text copyright © Penguin Books Ltd 1999
This edition copyright © Pearson Education Ltd 2008

Typeset by Graphicraft Ltd, Hong Kong
Set in 11/14pt Bembo
Printed in China
SWTC/04

Published by Pearson Education Ltd in association with
Penguin Books Ltd, both companies being subsidiaries of Pearson Plc

Contents

Introduction

Miranda, who thought all men had serious faces and grey beards like her father, was excited by the appearance of this beautiful young prince. And Ferdinand, seeing such a lovely lady in this empty place, thought he was on a magic island, and that Miranda was the goddess of the place. He began to address her with the respect a goddess deserves.

She answered, a little fearfully, that she was no goddess, but a simple girl . . .

Why does the Duke of Milan live alone on an island with his beautiful daughter – while another duke lives a simple but happy life in a forest? Why do two young people who hate each other suddenly fall in love, and another, loving young couple suddenly hate each other? Why does one man kill a friend to become king, and another man offer his life to bring a friend happiness? In these stories you will meet some of the most famous characters in world literature: Prospero and his beautiful daughter, Miranda; Oberon and Titania, the fairy king and queen; Shylock, the cruel moneylender; Macbeth, the murderous King of Scotland; Sebastian and Viola, the twins who look exactly the same. You will be taken on a journey to desert islands, magical forests, shadowy castles and sunlit palaces.

All of human experience can be found in Shakespeare – love, death, revenge, forgiveness, jealousy, friendship and greed – but the brilliance of his writing, the poetry of his language and the large number of complicated relationships in each play can make his work seem difficult to understand. In these stories, however, the humour, the magic, the moral doubts and the sad injustices of life are shown clearly, in a way that we can all easily recognize. We can share the characters' confusion and feel their happiness and their pain. In this way, we can enjoy the stories and at the same time ask ourselves the sometimes difficult questions about life that Shakespeare wants us to think about. If we can understand Shakespeare, we can understand as much about life as it is humanly possible to do.

These short stories open doors onto the beauty and brilliance of Shakespeare's universe, and make it easier for us to take the first step on a wonderful journey of exploration that can make our lives richer.

In 1807, Charles Lamb and his sister, Mary Lamb, were asked by their good friend William Goodwin to write the stories from the best-known of Shakespeare's plays in a form that children could easily understand. The stories were intended as an introduction to Shakespeare for readers who were too young to read the plays themselves. It was suggested that girls in particular, who were unable in those days to use libraries as freely as their brothers, would profit from them. The result was *Tales from Shakespeare*.

Charles and Mary chose twenty of Shakespeare's best-known plays and rewrote them in short-story form. Charles worked on the tragedies and Mary retold the comedies. In the introduction to their book, Charles and Mary explain their different methods of working. Charles's stories of the tragedies use much of Shakespeare's original language. The comedies, however, are more freely 'translated' from the original. Together, the Lambs managed to simplify Shakespeare's plays without losing their power or magic. Many people still believe that no better introduction to Shakespeare's work exists. 'I think it will be popular among the little people,' Charles wrote to a friend at the time. And he was right: the stories succeeded beyond expectation, enjoying popularity (with people of all sizes!) until the present day.

At the beginning of the nineteenth century, the moral tale was an important form of literature for children; stories were used mainly to teach children the difference between right and wrong. This affected the way that the Lambs wrote the stories: the characters are shown as either good or bad in a way that is less obvious in the plays, and the moral at the end of each story is very clear. The *Tales* attempt, wherever possible (especially in the tragedies, as we have seen), to use Shakespeare's own words to retell the stories, but the language is made easier. Some of the stories have also been made less complicated, with fewer characters than the originals.

For the Lambs, whose lives until this point had not been at all easy, the *Tales* were their first success in the world of literature. Charles was born in 1775, nine years after his sister, Mary Ann. Their father was a poorly paid lawyer's clerk in London. Charles was sent to the well-known Christ's Hospital School, but Mary, as a girl, did not have the opportunity for such a good education as her brother. For most of his life, Charles worked as a clerk at East India House, while writing in his free time. His work was not well paid and, although Mary earned a little money from needlework, the family was poor.

Mary gradually became mentally unbalanced, and then a terrible event took place that changed their lives forever. In 1796, their mother tried to stop a fight between Mary and another girl. The fight ended when Mary killed her mother with a knife. At the court case that followed, Mary was judged to be mentally ill and was sent to a mental home. But Charles managed to persuade the courts to let him take responsibility for looking after her, and she was allowed to return home after three years. Charles spent the rest of his life caring for her, and never married. Because it was known that she had murdered her mother and had been in a mental home, the pair had to move house several times. But they led a generally calm and happy life together and brought up a child called Emma Isola, who had no parents, as their daughter. Charles died in 1834, and Mary died thirteen years later.

Charles was a friend of many famous writers of his time,

including the poets Coleridge (whom he had first met at school), Wordsworth and Shelley. He was a respected and original judge of literature, who also wrote poems, plays and stories. With Mary, he wrote several books for children: they retold the story of the *Odyssey* in *The Adventures of Ulysses* (1808); *Mrs Leicester's School* (1809) and *Poetry for Children* (1809) followed.

William Shakespeare, whose plays are retold here in the form of short stories, is one of the world's greatest writers, but surprisingly little is known about his life, especially his early years in Stratford-upon-Avon. He was born on 23 April 1564. We know that his mother, Mary Arden, came from a higher social background than his father, John Shakespeare. He probably went to Stratford Grammar School, which offered free education to local boys, but did not attend university. In 1582, he married Anne Hathaway, and they had three children: Susanna, Hamnet and Judith.

From 1592 he was living in London, acting and writing plays. He became an important member of a theatre company which performed at two London theatres, the Globe and the Blackfriars. His plays were given special performances at the courts of Queen Elizabeth I and King James I, and his success made him a wealthy man. We know that he bought New Place, one of the largest houses in Stratford, for his family. He rebuilt the house, moved his wife and daughters there (his son had died in 1596), and spent his later years there himself when he left London. Shakespeare died on his fifty-second birthday, in 1616, and was buried in the church in Stratford.

Over a period of twenty-three years (1590–1613), Shakespeare wrote thirty-seven plays, sometimes writing three plays a year! His best-known plays include *A Midsummer Night's Dream* (1594), *Romeo and Juliet* (1595), *The Merchant of Venice* (1596), *Julius Caesar* (1599), *Hamlet* (1601), *Othello* (1604), *King Lear* (1605), *Macbeth* (1605) and *The Tempest* (1611). He also wrote much beautiful poetry.

Many of the stories in this collection are taken from plays written quite early in Shakespeare's professional life, between about 1595 and 1600 – the period in which he wrote his most joyful comedies. They share, therefore, many of Shakespeare's favourite ideas and situations. For example, *A Midsummer Night's Dream*, *Much Ado About Nothing* (1600), *As You Like It* (1599) and *Twelfth Night* (1600) are all light-hearted comedies involving the cruelties, misunderstandings and stormy emotions of young love. Characters with magical powers appear in *The Tempest*, *A Midsummer Night's Dream* and *Macbeth* (the only story in this collection written by Charles). The stories of *As You Like It*, *The Merchant of Venice* and *Macbeth*, and the much later story of *The Tempest*, all deal with the problems of forgiveness and revenge. The unusual and strange places in which the events take place all add to the wonder of the stories. Trickery and pretence play a big part in many of them, as characters compete against each other for personal gain, or from pure playfulness. But all the stories in this book (even the dark tragedy of *Macbeth*) end in a satisfying way, with love and goodness defeating evil and injustice.

Whether you are meeting Shakespeare for the first time, or are revisiting him, you will find these lovely stories by Charles and Mary Lamb very rewarding.

The Tempest

There was a certain island in the sea, on which there lived only an old man, whose name was Prospero, and his daughter Miranda, a very beautiful young lady.

They lived in a cave in a rock. It was divided into several parts, one of which Prospero called his study. There he kept his books, which mainly dealt with magic; and he found the knowledge of this art very useful to him. He had been thrown by a strange chance on this island, which had been put under a spell by a witch called Sycorax, and he had used the power of his art to set free many good spirits that Sycorax had shut up in the bodies of large trees, because they had refused to obey her evil commands. These gentle spirits were, after that, obedient to the will of Prospero. Of these spirits Ariel was the chief.

The bright little spirit Ariel had nothing bad in his nature, except that he took rather too much pleasure in troubling an ugly monster called Caliban, whom he disliked because he was the son of his old enemy Sycorax. Prospero had found this Caliban in the woods, a strange creature that looked far less like a man than a large monkey. Prospero took him home to his cave and taught him to speak and would have been very kind to him, but the bad nature which Caliban had from his mother, Sycorax, would not allow him to learn anything good or useful. So he was employed like a slave, to carry wood, and do the most tiring jobs; and Ariel had the duty of forcing him to carry out these services.

When Caliban was lazy and did not do his work, Ariel (who could be seen by no eyes except Prospero's) would come quietly up and take hold of him painfully, and sometimes throw him down in the mud; and then Ariel would take the form of a monkey, and make faces at him. With many cruel tricks like these Ariel would upset him, whenever Caliban failed to do the work which Prospero commanded him to do.

Having these powerful spirits obedient to his will, Prospero could by their means command the winds, and the waves of the sea. Following his orders they started a great storm, in the middle of which he showed his daughter a large ship struggling with the wild waves that every moment seemed about to swallow it up. The ship, he told her, was full of living beings like themselves.

'Oh, my dear father,' said she, 'if by your art you have brought this terrible storm, have pity on them. See! The ship will be broken to pieces, and they will all be drowned. If I had power, I would sink the sea beneath the earth, rather than destroy the good ship with all the poor people inside her.'

'Do not worry so, Miranda,' said Prospero; 'there is no harm done. I have ordered that no person in the ship shall receive any hurt. What I have done has been for you, my dear child. You do not know who you are, or where you came from, and you know no more of me except that I am your father and live in this poor cave. Can you remember a time before you came here? I think you cannot, for you were then not three years of age.'

'Certainly I can, sir,' replied Miranda. 'It seems to me like the memory of a dream. But did I not once have four or five women who served me?'

Prospero answered, 'You did, and more. How is it that this still lives in your mind? Do you remember how you came here?'

'No, sir,' said Miranda, 'I remember nothing more.'

◆

'Twelve years ago, Miranda,' continued Prospero, 'I was Duke of Milan, and you were a princess and my only child. I had a younger brother, whose name was Antonio, to whom I trusted everything; and as I was fond of quiet and deep study, I usually left the management of my state affairs to your uncle, my false brother (for so he proved). I, uninterested in all worldly aims, buried among my books, gave my whole time to the improvement of my mind. Since my brother Antonio was in possession of my power, he began to think that he was the duke. The opportunity I gave him of making himself popular among my subjects led him to the proud desire to rob me of my position. This he soon did with the help of the King of Naples, a powerful prince who was my enemy.'

'Why did they not destroy us then?' asked Miranda.

'My child,' answered her father, 'they dared not, so dear was the love that my people felt for me. Antonio carried us on board a ship, and when we were some miles out at sea, he forced us into a small boat, without either sails or ropes: there he left us, as he thought, to die. But a kind lord of my court, a man called Gonzalo, who loved me, had secretly placed in the boat water, food, clothing and some books which I value above my title.'

'Oh, my father,' said Miranda, 'what a trouble I must have been to you then!'

'No, my love,' said Prospero, 'you were the beautiful little creature whose smiles made me bear my misfortunes bravely. Our food lasted until we landed on this desert island; and since then my chief pleasure has been in teaching you, Miranda, and from these lessons you have learned well.'

'Heaven thank you, my dear father,' said Miranda. 'Now tell me, sir, your reason for ordering this storm?'

'I will,' said her father. 'By means of this storm, my enemies, the King of Naples and my cruel brother, are being driven on to this island.'

Having said this, Prospero gently touched his daughter with his magic stick, and she fell fast asleep; for the spirit Ariel just then appeared before his master, to give an account of the tempest, and of what he had done with the ship's company. Though the spirits could never be seen by Miranda, Prospero did not wish her to hear him speaking (as it would seem to her) to the empty air.

'Well, my brave spirit,' said Prospero to Ariel, 'how have you performed your work?'

Ariel gave a description of the storm, and of the fears of the sailors; and how the king's son, Ferdinand, was the first who jumped into the sea, and his father thought he saw his dear son swallowed up by the waves and lost.

'But he is safe,' said Ariel, 'in a corner of the island, sitting with his arms folded, crying for the loss of the king, his father, whom he believes has been drowned. Not a hair of his head has been hurt, and his princely clothes, though wet from the waves of the sea, look fresher than before.'

'That's my delicate Ariel,' said Prospero. 'Bring him here: my daughter must see this young prince. Where is the king, and my brother?'

'I left them,' answered Ariel, 'searching for Ferdinand, whom they have little hope of finding. Of the sailors not one is missing, though each one thinks himself the only one saved; and the ship, though out of sight, is safe in the port.'

'Ariel,' said Prospero, 'you have done your work well, but there is more to do.'

'Is there more work?' said Ariel. 'Let me remind you, master, you have promised me my freedom. I have served you well and without complaint, told you no lies, made no mistakes.'

'What?' said Prospero. 'You do not remember what pain I freed you from. Have you forgotten the evil witch Sycorax, who was almost bent double with age and jealousy? Where was she born? Speak; tell me.'

'Sir, in Algiers,' said Ariel.

'Oh, was she?' said Prospero. 'I must remind you of things that I find you have forgotten. This witch, Sycorax, was driven from Algiers for the things she did, too terrible for human ears, and was left here by the sailors; and because you were a spirit too delicate to carry out her evil commands, she shut you up in a tree, where I found you crying. This pain, remember, I freed you from.'

'Pardon me, dear master,' said Ariel, ashamed to seem ungrateful. 'I will obey your commands.'

'Do so,' said Prospero, 'and I will set you free.' He then gave more orders, and away went Ariel. First the spirit went to where he had left Ferdinand, and found him still sitting on the grass in the same sad state.

'Oh, my young gentleman,' said Ariel, when he saw him, 'I will soon move you. You must be brought, I find, for the Lady Miranda to have a sight of your pretty figure. Come, sir, follow me.'

He began to sing, and the prince followed the magic sound of Ariel's voice until it led him to Prospero and Miranda, who were sitting under the shade of a large tree. Now Miranda had never seen a man before, except her own father.

'Miranda,' said Prospero, 'tell me what you are looking at over there.'

'Oh, father,' said Miranda, in surprise, 'surely that is a spirit. Believe me, sir, it is a beautiful creature. Is it not a spirit?'

'No, girl,' answered her father, 'it eats, and sleeps, and has senses just as we have. This young man you see was on the ship. He is rather changed by grief, or you might call him beautiful. He has lost his companions, and is wandering about to find them.'

Miranda, who thought all men had serious faces and grey beards like her father, was excited by the appearance of this beautiful young prince. And Ferdinand, seeing such a lovely lady in this empty place, thought he was on a magic island, and that Miranda was the goddess of the place. He began to address her with the respect a goddess deserves.

She answered, a little fearfully, that she was no goddess, but a simple girl, and was going to give him an account of herself, when Prospero interrupted her. He was well pleased to find they admired each other; he saw clearly they had (as we say) fallen in love at first sight. To test Ferdinand's love, though, he decided to throw some difficulties in their way; stepping forward, he addressed the prince severely, telling him he came to the island as a thief, to steal it from its real master, himself.

'Follow me,' said Prospero. 'I will tie you up. You shall drink seawater; shellfish and dead roots shall be your food.'

'No,' said Ferdinand. 'I will fight against that kind of entertainment until I see a more powerful enemy.' He pulled out his sword; but Prospero, waving his magic stick, fixed him to the spot where he stood, so that he had no power to move.

Miranda ran to her father, saying, 'Why are you so unkind? Have pity, sir. This is the second man I have ever seen, and to me he seems a true one.'

◆

'Silence,' said the father, 'one more word will make me angry with you, girl! What! Will you speak for a thief? You think there are no finer men, because you have seen only him and Caliban.'

He said this to test his daughter's love; and she replied, 'I have no wish to see a finer man.'

'Come on, young man,' said Prospero to the prince, 'you have no power to disobey me.'

'I have not,' answered Ferdinand; and not knowing that it was by magic he was robbed of all power to fight, he was surprised to find himself so strangely forced to follow Prospero. Looking back on Miranda as long as he could see her, he said, as he went after Prospero into the cave, 'I feel as if I were in a dream; but this man's threats, and the weakness which I feel, would be nothing if I could see this fair young woman once a day from my prison.'

Prospero did not keep Ferdinand shut up long inside the cave. He soon brought out his prisoner and gave him a difficult job, taking care to let his daughter know what he had done. Then, pretending to go into his study, he secretly watched them both.

Prospero had commanded Ferdinand to pile up some heavy pieces of wood. Kings' sons are not used to hard physical work, so Miranda soon found her lover almost dying with tiredness.

'Oh, sir!' said she, 'do not work so hard; my father is at his studies, and will not come out for at least three hours. Please rest yourself.'

'Oh, my dear lady,' said Ferdinand, 'I dare not. I must finish my job before I rest.'

'If you will sit down,' said Miranda, 'I will carry your wood for a little while.' But Ferdinand would not agree to this. Instead of helping Ferdinand with his work, Miranda prevented him from doing it, since they began a long conversation and the business of wood-carrying went on very slowly.

Prospero, who had given Ferdinand this job as a test of his love, was not at his books, as his daughter thought, but was standing near them unseen, to hear what they said.

Ferdinand asked her name, which she told him, saying that she did so against her father's command.

Prospero only smiled at this first example of his daughter's disobedience; having, by his magic art, caused his daughter to fall in love so suddenly, he was not angry that she showed her love by forgetting to obey his commands. And he listened with pleasure to a long speech of Ferdinand's, in which he said he loved her more than any lady he had ever seen.

In answer to his praises of her beauty, which he said was greater than any other woman's in the world, she replied, 'I do not remember the face of any woman, nor have I seen any more men than you, my good friend, and my dear father. But, believe me, sir, I would not wish for any companion in the world except you, nor can my imagination form any shape that I could like more than yours. But, sir, I fear I am talking to you too freely, and I am forgetting my father's commands.'

At this Prospero smiled to himself, as much as to say, 'This is going exactly as I wished; my girl will be Queen of Naples.'

And then Ferdinand, in another fine long speech (for young princes speak in courtly language), told the sweet Miranda that he would be the next king of Naples, and that she should be his queen.

'Ah, sir,' said she, 'I am a fool to cry at what I am glad of. I will be your wife, if you wish to marry me.'

Before Ferdinand could thank her, Prospero appeared before them.

'Fear nothing, my child,' said he. 'I have heard and approve of all you have said. And Ferdinand, if I have used you too severely, I will pay you well by giving you my daughter. All your troubles were only tests of your love, and you have stood the tests well. So take my daughter as my gift, which your true love has bought, and do not smile when I tell you she is above all praise.'

Then, telling them that he had business in another place, he asked them to sit down and talk together, until he returned; and this command Miranda seemed unlikely to disobey.

◆

When Prospero left them, he called his spirit Ariel, who quickly appeared before him, eager to tell him what he had done with Prospero's brother and the King of Naples. Ariel said he had left them almost out of their senses with fear at the strange things he had caused them to see and hear. When they were tired of wandering about, and half dead for want of food, he had suddenly set a fine meal in front of them. And then, just as they were going to eat, he had appeared before them in the shape of a hungry monster with wings, and the meal had disappeared. Then, to their great surprise, this monster spoke to them, reminding them of their cruelty in driving Prospero from his own country, and leaving him and his little daughter to die at sea; for this reason, they were now suffering these terrors.

The King of Naples and Antonio, the false brother, were filled with sorrow for the injustice they had done to Prospero, and Ariel told his master he was certain their guilt was sincere, and that he, though a spirit, could not help pitying them.

'Then bring them here, Ariel,' said Prospero. 'If you, who are only a spirit, feel for their grief, surely I, who am a human being like themselves, will have pity on them. Bring them quickly, my pretty Ariel.'

Ariel soon returned with the king, Antonio and old Gonzalo. They had followed him, trapped by the wild music he played in the air to lead them to his master's presence. This Gonzalo was the same man who had so kindly provided Prospero with books and food, when his evil brother had left him to die in an open boat at sea.

Grief and terror had so deadened the senses of the three men that they did not know Prospero. He first made himself known to good old Gonzalo, calling him his life-saver; and then his brother and the king realized that he was the Prospero they had tried to kill.

Antonio, with tears of sorrow and true shame, begged his brother's forgiveness, and the king said he, too, was sorry that he had helped Antonio to take his brother's place. And Prospero forgave them; and when they promised to give back his title and property, he said to the King of Naples, 'I have a gift for you, too'; and opening a door, Prospero showed him his son Ferdinand with Miranda.

Nothing could have been greater than the joy of the father and the son at this unexpected meeting, since they each thought that the other had been drowned in the storm.

'Oh, heavens!' said Miranda. 'What lovely creatures these are! It must surely be a fine world that has such people in it.'

The King of Naples was almost as surprised at the beauty of Miranda as his son had been. 'Who is this young woman?' said he. 'She must be the goddess that has parted us and has brought us together.'

'No, sir,' answered Ferdinand, smiling to find his father had made the same mistake that he had made when he first saw Miranda, 'she is only a woman, but by God's goodness she is mine. I chose her when I could not ask you, my father, for your permission, not knowing you were alive. She is the daughter of this Prospero, who is the Duke of Milan, of whose fame I have heard so much. I have never seen him until now, but from him I have received a new life; he has made himself my second father by giving me this dear lady.'

'Then I must be her father,' said the king, 'but oh, how strange it will sound when I ask my own child's forgiveness.'

'No more of that,' said Prospero. 'Let us not remember our past troubles, since they have ended so happily.' And then

Prospero kissed his brother, and gave him his forgiveness again. He said that a wise, all-powerful God had allowed him to be driven from his home in Milan so that his daughter could become Queen of Naples, since through their meeting on this desert island it had happened that the king's son had fallen in love with Miranda.

These kind words which Prospero spoke, meaning to comfort his brother, filled Antonio with such shame and sorrow that he cried and was unable to speak. And the kind old Gonzalo also cried to see this joyful union of hearts, and prayed for the young people's happiness.

Prospero now told them that their ship was safe in the port, and the sailors were all on board, and that he and his daughter would go home with them the next morning.

'But now,' said he, 'let's share whatever food my poor cave can provide; and for your evening's entertainment I will tell you the history of my life from my first landing on this desert island.' He then called for Caliban to prepare some food and set the cave in order. The company were shocked at the strange form and wild appearance of this ugly monster, who (Prospero said) was the only servant he had to help him.

Before Prospero left the island, he dismissed Ariel from his service, to the great joy of that little spirit. Although he had been a good servant to his master, he was always longing to enjoy his freedom, to wander uncontrolled in the air, like a wild bird, under green trees, among pleasant fruits and sweet-smelling flowers.

'My pretty Ariel,' said Prospero to the little spirit when he set him free, 'I shall miss you; but you can have your freedom.'

'Thank you, my dear master,' said Ariel. 'But allow me to help your ship home with favourable winds, before you say goodbye to your honest spirit. And then, master, when I am free, how happily I shall live!'

Prospero buried his magical books and his stick deep in the earth, because he was determined never more to make use of the magic art. And having defeated his enemies, and being united with his brother and the King of Naples, nothing now remained to complete his happiness, except to revisit his homeland, to take possession of Milan, and to witness the happy marriage of his daughter Miranda and Prince Ferdinand, which the king said should be celebrated immediately after their return to Naples. And, after a pleasant journey, and under the protection of the spirit Ariel, they soon arrived there.

A Midsummer Night's Dream

CHARACTERS
Theseus, Duke of Athens
Egeus, a citizen of Athens
Demetrius, a young Athenian
Lysander
A country man
Hermia, daughter of Egeus
Helena, her friend
Oberon, king of the fairies
Titania, queen of the fairies
Puck, adviser to Oberon
Fairies, serving Titania

There was a law in the city of Athens which gave its citizens the power to force their daughters to marry whoever they pleased. If a daughter refused to marry the man her father had chosen to be her husband, the father could by this law cause her to be killed. But as fathers do not often desire the death of their own daughters, even if they are a little disobedient, this law was rarely or never used.

But there was one case of an old man, whose name was Egeus, who actually did come to Theseus (at that time the Duke of Athens), to make a complaint about his daughter Hermia. He had commanded Hermia to marry Demetrius, a young man of an old Athenian family, but she refused to obey him, because she loved another young Athenian, named Lysander. Egeus demanded justice from Theseus, and asked for this cruel law to be used against his daughter.

Hermia's defence was that Demetrius had formerly said that he loved her dear friend Helena, and that Helena loved Demetrius deeply. But this good reason which Hermia gave for not obeying her father's command did not move the severe Egeus at all.

Theseus, though a great and good prince, had no power to change the laws of his country. So he could only give Hermia four days to consider the matter; at the end of that time, if she still refused to marry Demetrius, she would be put to death.

When Hermia left the presence of the duke, she went to her lover Lysander. She told him the danger she was in, and that she must either give him up and marry Demetrius, or lose her life in four days' time.

Lysander was terribly upset when he heard this news. But remembering that he had an aunt who lived at some distance from Athens, and that at the place where she lived the cruel law could not be used against Hermia, he suggested to his lover that she should secretly leave her father's house that night, and go with him to his aunt's house, where he would marry her.

'I will meet you,' said Lysander, 'in the wood a few miles outside the city; in that happy wood where we have so often walked with Helena.'

Hermia joyfully agreed to this suggestion, and she told no one of her intended flight except her friend Helena. As young women do foolish things for love, Helena decided to go and tell this to Demetrius; she could hope to gain nothing by giving away her friend's secret, except the small pleasure of following the man she loved to the wood, because she knew that Demetrius would in fact go there after Hermia.

◆

The wood in which Lysander and Hermia planned to meet was the favourite meeting-place of those little beings known as fairies.

14

Oberon the king, and Titania the queen of the fairies, with their company of little followers, held their midnight dances in this wood.

Between this little king and queen of the fairies there was, at this time, a sad disagreement. They never met by moonlight in the shady walks of this pleasant wood without quarrelling, until all their followers ran away and hid themselves in fear.

The cause of this unhappy disagreement was Titania's refusal to give Oberon a little boy as his servant. The boy's mother had been Titania's friend, and on her death the fairy queen stole the child from its nurse, and brought him up in the woods.

The night on which the lovers were to meet in this wood, Titania was walking with some of her servants, when she met Oberon with his company of fairy followers.

'What, jealous Oberon, is it you?' the fairy queen cried. 'Fairies, run away; I have sworn to avoid his company.'

'Wait, foolish fairy,' said Oberon. 'Am I not your lord? Why do you oppose me so? Give me that little boy to serve me.'

'Set your heart at rest,' answered the queen, angrily. 'Your whole fairy kingdom will not buy the boy from me.'

'Well, go on your way,' said Oberon. 'Before the morning comes, I will make you suffer for this injury that you have done me.'

Oberon then sent for Puck, his favourite fairy and adviser.

Puck was a clever fairy who enjoyed playing tricks on farm girls in the neighbouring villages: sometimes taking the cream from the milk, sometimes throwing his light and airy form into the butter machine and preventing the cream from changing into butter. Nor did the village men have any better luck: whenever Puck chose to play his games in the beer pan, the beer was sure to be spoiled. When a few good neighbours met to drink some beer together, Puck would jump into the bowl of beer in the likeness of some animal or other, and when an old woman was going to drink, he would jump against her lips, and the beer would run down her old chin. And soon after that, when the same old woman was seating herself to tell her neighbours a sad story, Puck would pull her seat from under her, and the poor old thing would fall down, and then the other old women would hold their sides and laugh at her and swear they had never spent a more amusing hour.

'Come here, Puck,' said Oberon to this little wanderer of the night. 'Bring me the little purple flower, the juice from which, laid on the eyelids of those who sleep, will make them love deeply the first thing they see when they awake. I will drop some of the juice of that flower on the eyelids of my Titania when she is asleep and she will fall in love with the first thing she looks at when she opens her eyes, even if it's a lion, a bear, or a monkey. And before I take this magic spell away, which I can do with another spell, I will make her give me that boy to be my servant.'

Puck, who dearly loved such games, was highly pleased with his master's joke, and ran to search for the flower. While Oberon was waiting for Puck's return, he saw Demetrius and Helena enter the woods. He heard Demetrius complaining to Helena that she should not have followed him; after many unkind words on his part, and gentle replies from Helena, reminding him of his former love and promises to her, he left her (as he said) to the mercy of the wild animals, and she ran after him as quickly as she could.

The fairy king, who was always friendly to true lovers, felt great pity for Helena. So when Puck returned with the little purple flower, Oberon said to his favourite, 'There has been a sweet Athenian lady here, who is in love with a cruel youth. Take a part of this flower and, if you find him sleeping, drop some of the love-juice in his eyes. But make sure that you do it when she is near him, so that the first thing he sees when he wakes is this lady. You will know the man by the Athenian clothes which he wears.' Puck promised to do this very carefully; and then Oberon went, unseen by Titania, to her resting place, where she was preparing to go to sleep. This was a bank, where many kinds of sweetly smelling, prettily coloured wild flowers grew under a roof of climbing roses. There Titania always slept for some part of the night; her bedcover was a snake skin, which, though a small thing, was wide enough to wrap a fairy in.

He found Titania giving orders to her fairies about how they were to busy themselves while she slept. 'Some of you,' said Titania, 'must kill the insects that eat the young rose flowers; and some must attack the bats for their leather wings, to make my small fairy coats; and some of you must keep watch to make sure that the noisy birds do not come near me. But first, sing me to sleep.'

When the fairies had sung their queen to sleep, they left her to perform the important services she had given them. Oberon then came softly up to his Titania and dropped some of the love-juice on her eyelids, saying, 'What you see when you wake – that will be your true love.'

◆

But we must return to Hermia. She escaped from her father's house that night, to avoid the death that she faced for refusing to marry Demetrius. When she entered the wood, she found her dear Lysander waiting for her to take her to his aunt's house. But before they were halfway through the wood, Hermia was so tired that Lysander made her rest until morning on the soft green bank. And lying down himself on the ground at some little distance, they soon fell fast asleep.

Here they were found by Puck. Puck saw a good-looking young man asleep, and noticed that his clothes were made in the Athenian way and that a pretty lady was sleeping near him; he thought, therefore, that this must be the Athenian girl and her

17

cruel lover whom Oberon had sent him to find. And he naturally enough supposed that, as they were alone together, she would be the first thing he would see when he awoke; so, without delay, he poured some of the juice of the little purple flower into his eyes. But it happened that Helena came that way, and, instead of Hermia, she was the first thing Lysander saw when he opened his eyes. And strange to say, so powerful was the love-spell that all his love for Hermia disappeared, and Lysander fell in love with Helena.

If he had seen Hermia first when he awoke, the mistake Puck made would not have mattered, since he could not love that lady too well. But for poor Lysander to be forced by a fairy love-spell to forget his own true Hermia, and to run after another lady and leave Hermia asleep alone in a wood at midnight, was very sad.

◆

The misfortune happened in this way. Helena tried to keep up with Demetrius when he ran away from her so rudely, but she could not continue this unequal race for long, since men are always better runners in a long race than women. So Helena soon lost sight of Demetrius; and while she was wandering around in a sad and lonely way, she arrived at the place where Lysander was sleeping.

'Ah!' said she. 'This is Lysander lying on the ground. Is he dead or asleep?' Then, gently touching him, she said, 'Good sir, if you are alive, awake.'

Lysander opened his eyes, and, as the love-juice began to work, immediately spoke to Helena words of the wildest love and admiration; he told her that her beauty was even greater than Hermia's, and that he would run through fire for her. Helena, knowing Lysander was her friend Hermia's lover, and that he had promised to marry her, was very angry when she heard herself addressed in this manner; she thought (as one can imagine) that

Lysander was making a fool of her.

'Oh!' she said angrily. 'Why was I born to be laughed at by everyone? Is it not enough, is it not enough, young man, that I can never get a sweet look or a kind word from Demetrius? Must you now, sir, must you pretend in this cruel manner to love me? I thought, Lysander, you were too kind for that.' She ran away, and Lysander followed her, completely forgetting his own Hermia, who was still asleep.

◆

When Hermia awoke, she was sad and frightened at finding herself alone. She wandered through the wood, not knowing what had happened to Lysander, or which way to go in search of him. While this was happening, Demetrius, not being able to find Hermia and his rival Lysander, and tired after his useless search, fell asleep and was found by Oberon. Oberon had learnt, as a result of some questions he had asked Puck, that his helper had put the love-juice in the wrong person's eyes. Since Oberon had now found the person he had intended to help, he touched the eyes of the sleeping Demetrius with the love-juice. The young man woke immediately; and since the first thing he saw was Helena, he, like Lysander before him, began to make loving speeches to her. Just at that moment Lysander made his appearance, followed by Hermia (because of Puck's unlucky mistake, it was now Hermia's turn to run after her lover). Then Lysander and Demetrius, both speaking at the same time, and each in the power of the same strong spell, begged Helena to pity the strength of their love for her.

The shocked Helena thought that Demetrius, Lysander, and her once dear friend Hermia, had planned together to make a fool of her.

But Hermia was as surprised as Helena: she did not know why Lysander and Demetrius, who had both loved her before, had now become Helena's lovers; and to Hermia the affair seemed to be no laughing matter. The ladies, who had always been the dearest of friends, now exchanged angry words.

'Unkind Hermia,' said Helena, 'it is you who have persuaded Lysander to trouble me with pretended praises; and your other lover Demetrius, who used to hate me, have you not told him to call me a heavenly goddess? He would not speak like this, if you had not encouraged him to make a fool of me. Unkind Hermia, to join with men in laughing at your poor friend. Have you forgotten when we were schoolfriends? How often, Hermia, have we two, sitting on one seat, singing one song, with our needles sewing the same flower, both worked on the same cloth? We have grown up together like twins, and rarely been parted. Hermia, it is not kind of you to join with men in laughing at your poor friend.'

'I do not understand your angry words,' said Hermia. 'I am not laughing at you; it seems, though, that you are laughing at me.'

'Continue, then,' replied Helena. 'Pretend serious looks, and make faces at me when I turn my back; then smile at each other. If you had any pity or manners, you would not treat me like this.'

While Helena and Hermia were speaking these angry words to each other, Demetrius and Lysander left them. The young men went off to fight for the love of Helena. The ladies found the gentlemen had gone, and wandered in the wood once more in search of their lovers.

As soon as they were gone, the fairy king, who with little Puck had been listening to their quarrels, said to him, 'This is your carelessness, Puck; or did you do it purposely?'

'Believe me, king of shadows,' answered Puck, 'it was a mistake; did you not tell me I would know the man from his Athenian clothes? But I am not sorry this has happened, because I am greatly enjoying their quarrelling.'

'You heard,' said Oberon, 'that Demetrius and Lysander have gone to look for a place to fight in. I command you to fill the night with cloud and mist, and to lead these quarrelling lovers so far from one another in the dark that they will not be able to find each other. Do this until they are so tired they can go no further; and when you find they are asleep, drop the juice of this other flower into Lysander's eyes. When he wakes he will forget his new love for Helena, and return to his old love for Hermia; and then the two fair ladies will each be happy with the man she loves, and they will think everything that has passed has been an ugly dream. Do this quickly, Puck, and I will go and see what sweet love my Titania has found.'

◆

Titania was still sleeping, and Oberon saw a farm worker near her, who had lost his way in the wood and was also asleep. 'This fool,' said he, 'shall be my Titania's true love'; and putting an ass's head over the countryman's, he made it fit him as well as if it had grown on his own shoulders. Though Oberon fixed the ass's head on very gently, it woke the man. He got up, not knowing what Oberon had done to him, and went towards the resting-place where the fairy queen was sleeping.

'Ah! What beautiful creature is this?' said Titania, as she opened her eyes and the juice of the little purple flower began to take effect. 'Are you as wise as you are beautiful?'

'Well, madam,' said the foolish creature with the ass's head, 'if I have wisdom enough to find my way out of this wood, I have enough to serve my purpose.'

'Do not desire to go out of the wood,' said the lovesick queen. 'I love you. I am a spirit of no common kind. Come with me and I will give you fairies to serve you.'

She then called four of her fairies, whose names were Pease-blossom, Cobweb, Moth and Mustard-seed.

'Look after this sweet gentleman,' ordered the queen. 'Go with him on his walks, and play in his sight and feed him with fruit. Come, sit with me,' she said to him, 'and let me play with your pretty hairy cheeks, my beautiful ass, and kiss your lovely large ears, my gentle joy!'

'Where is Pease-blossom?' said the ass-headed fool, not paying much attention to the fairy queen's love, but very proud of his new servants.

'Here, sir,' said little Pease-blossom.

'Scratch my head,' said he. 'Where is Cobweb?'

'Here, sir,' said Cobweb.

'Good Mr Cobweb,' said he, 'please bring me some fruit. Where is Mustard-seed?'

'Here, sir,' said Mustard-seed, 'what is your wish?'

'Nothing, good Mr Mustard-seed,' said the fool, 'but to help Mr Pease-blossom to scratch. I must have my hair cut, Mr Mustard-seed, as I think I am extremely hairy about the face.'

'My sweet love,' said the queen, 'what will you have to eat? I have a fairy who can bring you some fresh nuts.'

'I would rather have a handful of dried grass,' said the man who with his ass's head had developed an ass's taste. 'But let none of your people trouble me now, because I would like to sleep.'

'Sleep, then,' said the queen, 'and I will hold you in my arms. Oh, how I love you! How I love you!'

When the fairy king saw the creature sleeping in the arms of the queen, he showed himself to her and complained that she was showing kindness to an ass.

This she had to agree to, as the fool was at that moment sleeping in her arms, with his ass's head crowned by her with flowers.

When Oberon had laughed at her for some time, he again demanded the boy; and she, ashamed of being found by her lord with her new favourite, did not dare to refuse him.

Now that Oberon had the little boy he had wished for for so long to be his servant, he took pity on his Titania, and threw some of the juice of the other flower into her eyes. The fairy queen immediately came to her senses, and could not believe her recent foolishness. She protested that she now hated the sight of the strange monster.

Oberon then took the ass's head away from the poor creature, and left him to finish his sleep with his own fool's head on his shoulders.

Since Oberon and his Titania were now perfectly reunited, he told her the history of the lovers and their midnight quarrels, and she agreed to go with him to see the end of their adventures.

◆

The fairy king and queen found the lovers and their fair ladies at no great distance from each other, sleeping on a piece of grass. To repay them for his former mistake, Puck had very carefully brought them all to the same spot, unknown to each other; and he had carefully removed the spell from Lysander's eyes with the medicine Oberon had given to him.

Hermia awoke first and, seeing her lost Lysander asleep so near her, thought about the strangeness of his sudden loss of love for her. Lysander soon opened his eyes, saw again with the eyes which the fairy-spell had clouded, and rediscovered his love for Hermia. And they began to talk over the adventures of the night, wondering if these things had really happened, or if they had both been dreaming the same confusing dream.

Helena and Demetrius were awake by this time; and since a sweet sleep had quieted Helena's troubled and angry mind, she listened with pleasure to the words of love which Demetrius still spoke to her, and which, to her surprise as well as pleasure, she saw were truly meant.

These fair night-wandering ladies, now no longer rivals,

became true friends again. All the unkind words which had passed between them were forgiven, and they calmly planned together what was best to be done in their present condition. It was soon agreed that, as Demetrius had given up his claim to Hermia, he should try to persuade her father to remove the cruel sentence of death which had been passed against her. Demetrius was preparing to return to Athens for this purpose, when they were surprised to see Egeus, Hermia's father, who had come to the wood to find his runaway daughter.

When Egeus understood that Demetrius would not now marry his daughter, he no longer opposed her marriage with Lysander, but gave his permission that they should be joined together on the fourth day from that time (the same day on which Hermia had been told she would lose her life). And on that same day Helena joyfully agreed to marry her Demetrius.

The fairy king and queen, who were present at this happy ending, though unseen, were so pleased that they honoured the marriages with sports and games throughout their fairy kingdom.

And now, if anyone is offended by this story of fairies and their tricks, judging it strange and beyond belief, they only have to imagine that they have been asleep, and that all these adventures took place in their dreams.

Much Ado About Nothing

CHARACTERS
Leonato, Governor of Messina
Pedro, Prince of Aragon
Claudio, a lord of Florence
Benedick, a lord of Padua
John, half-brother of Pedro
Borachio
A priest
Hero, daughter of Leonato
Beatrice, niece of Leonato
Margaret and Ursula, women serving Hero

There lived in the palace at Messina two ladies, whose names were Hero and Beatrice. Hero was the daughter, and Beatrice the niece, of Leonato, the Governor of Messina.

Beatrice was an active, fun-loving person, and liked to amuse her cousin Hero, who was more serious, with her clever talk. Whatever was happening was sure to be the cause of laughter for the light-hearted Beatrice.

At the time when this story begins, some young army officers came to visit Leonato. Among these were Pedro, the Prince of Aragon, and his friend Claudio, who was a lord of Florence; and with them came the wild and amusing Benedick, who was a lord of Padua. These strangers had been at Messina before, and the governor presented them to his daughter and his niece as old friends.

The moment he entered the room, Benedick began a loud conversation with Leonato and the prince. Beatrice, who did not like to be left out of any conversation, interrupted Benedick by saying, 'I'm surprised that you are still talking, Signor* Benedick, since nobody is listening to you.'

Benedick was just as fun-loving as Beatrice, but he was not pleased by this remark. He did not approve of a lady being so free with her tongue; and he remembered that when he was last at Messina, Beatrice used to choose him to play her tricks on. And as there is no one who so little likes to be laughed at as those who like to laugh at others, Benedick and Beatrice were always equally displeased with each other when they parted. So when Beatrice stopped him in the middle of his speech and told him that nobody was listening to what he was saying, Benedick, pretending not to have noticed before that she was present, said, 'What, my dear lady, are you still alive?' And war broke out again between them. Beatrice knew that he had proved his courage in a recent battle, but said that she would eat everything he had killed there; seeing the prince take pleasure in Benedick's conversation, she also called him 'the prince's jester'. This hurt Benedick more deeply than anything Beatrice had said before. There is nothing that people who think they are funny fear so much as the charge that they are jesters, because that is sometimes a little too near the truth.

◆

The lady Hero was silent in front of the guests. While Claudio was carefully examining the improvement in her beauty, and her fine figure (for she was a very attractive young lady), the prince was listening with pleasure to the sharp conversation between Benedick and Beatrice; and he said in a whisper to Leonato, 'This is a pleasant-spirited young lady. She would be an excellent wife for Benedick.' Leonato replied, 'Oh, my lord, my lord, if they

* Signor: the Italian word for Mr.

were only married for a week, they would talk themselves crazy.' But though Leonato thought they would make a strange pair, the prince did not give up the idea of matching these two together.

When Pedro left the palace with Claudio, he found that the marriage he had planned between Benedick and Beatrice was not the only one that had been thought of there. Claudio spoke of Hero in such a way that the prince guessed at what was in his heart. He approved, so he asked Claudio, 'Are you thinking about Hero?' To this question Claudio replied, 'Oh, my lord, when I was last at Messina I liked her, but had no time for loving; now, in this happy time of peace, thoughts of war have left my mind, and soft and pleasant thoughts are crowding in their place, all telling me how attractive young Hero is, reminding me that I liked her before I went to war.' These words of Claudio's moved the prince so much that he lost no time in asking Leonato to accept Claudio as his daughter's husband. Leonato agreed, and the prince had no great difficulty in persuading the gentle Hero herself to listen to Claudio, who was a wise and gifted man. Helped by his kind prince, Claudio soon persuaded Leonato to fix an early day for his marriage with Hero.

He had to wait only a few days before his wedding, but he complained that it seemed a long time. So to make the time pass more quickly, the prince suggested, as a kind of game, that they should think of a clever plan to make Benedick and Beatrice fall in love with each other. Claudio was happy to agree to Pedro's strange idea; Leonato promised them his help, and even Hero said she would do anything she could to help her cousin to find a good husband.

◆

The prince's plan was that the gentlemen should make Benedick believe that Beatrice was in love with him, and Hero should make Beatrice believe that Benedick was in love with her.

The prince, Leonato and Claudio started work first. Finding their opportunity when Benedick was quietly reading in the garden, the prince and his helpers took up their position among the trees, so near that Benedick could not help hearing all they said. After some talk on other subjects, the prince said, 'Tell me, Leonato. What was it you said to me the other day – that your niece Beatrice was in love with Benedick? I did not think that lady would have loved any man.'

'No, nor I, my lord,' answered Leonato. 'It is interesting that she should love Benedick so much, when she always seems to dislike him.'

Claudio then said that Hero had told him Beatrice was so in love with Benedick that she would certainly die of grief if he could not be persuaded to love her. Leonato and Claudio seemed to agree that that was impossible, though, since Benedick had always spoken against all attractive ladies, and in particular against Beatrice.

The prince pretended to feel great pity for Beatrice as he listened to this, and he said, 'It would be good if Benedick were told about this.'

'Why?' said Claudio. 'He would only make fun of her, and upset the poor lady even more.'

'And if he did,' said the prince, 'he would be in trouble. Beatrice is a lovely lady, and very wise in everything but in loving Benedick.'

Then the prince signalled to his companions that they should walk, and leave Benedick to think about what he had heard.

◆

Benedick had been listening with great eagerness to this conversation; and when he heard Beatrice loved him, he said to himself, 'Is it possible? Can it be true? Is that the way the wind blows?'

And when they had gone, he began to reason with himself: 'This cannot be a trick! They were very serious, and they have the truth from Hero and seem to pity the lady. Love me! Then her love must be returned! I never thought I would marry. But they say the lady is lovely – and wise in everything but loving me. Well, that is no great proof of her foolishness. But here comes Beatrice. Yes, it is true, she is an attractive lady.'

Beatrice now came towards him, and said with her usual sharpness, 'I have been sent against my will to ask you to come in to dinner.'

Benedick, who had never felt himself able to speak so politely to her before, replied, 'Fair Beatrice, I thank you for your trouble.' When Beatrice left him, after two or three more rude remarks, Benedick thought he had noticed a hidden kindness under her hard words, and he said to himself, 'If I do not take pity on her and love her, I am an evil man.'

◆

Since the gentleman was now caught in the net they had spread for him, it was Hero's turn to play her part with Beatrice. And for this purpose she sent for Ursula and Margaret, two women who served her, and she said to Margaret, 'Good Margaret, run to the sitting room; there you will find my cousin Beatrice talking to the prince and Claudio. Whisper in her ear that Ursula and I are walking in the garden, and that we are talking about her. Tell her to come and listen.'

'I will make her come immediately, I promise you,' said Margaret.

Hero then took Ursula with her into the garden, and said to her, 'Now, Ursula, when Beatrice comes, we will walk up and down this path, and our conversation will only be about Benedick, and when I name him, you must praise him more than any man has ever deserved. I shall be telling you that Benedick is in love with Beatrice. Now begin – look over there where Beatrice is running towards us to hear our conversation.'

They then began, Hero saying, as if in answer to something which Ursula had said, 'No, truly, Ursula. She is too proud; she is as shy as a wild bird.'

'But are you sure,' said Ursula, 'that Signor Benedick loves Beatrice so completely?'

'So the prince says,' Hero replied. 'And my lord Claudio. They begged me to tell her; but I persuaded them, if they loved Benedick, never to let Beatrice know of it.'

'Certainly,' replied Ursula, 'it would not be a good thing for her to know about his love, in case she made fun of it.'

'Exactly,' said Hero. 'I have never yet seen a man, wise, young, or beautiful, whom she would not find fault with.'

'Such cruel judgements are not good,' said Ursula.

'No,' replied Hero, 'but who would dare to tell her so? If I spoke, she would just laugh at me.'

'Oh, you wrong your cousin,' said Ursula. 'She cannot be so lacking true judgement as to refuse so fine a gentleman as Signor Benedick.'

'He has an excellent name,' said Hero. 'In fact, he is the first man in Italy, except for my dear Claudio.'

Hero then told Ursula that she was going to be married to Claudio the next day, and asked her to go in with her and look at some new clothes, as she wished to ask her advice about what she should wear.

When they went away, Beatrice, who had been listening very eagerly to this talk, cried out, 'Can this be true? Benedick, love on! I will repay you, and soften my wild heart under your loving hand.'

It must have been a pleasant sight to see these old enemies turned into new and loving friends, and to see their first meeting after being tricked into liking one another by the plan of the good-natured prince. But now came a sad change in the fortunes of Hero. The next day, which should have been her wedding day, brought sorrow to the hearts of both Hero and her good father Leonato.

◆

The prince had a half-brother, who came back with him from the wars to Messina. This brother (whose name was John) was a sad man who seemed to enjoy the planning of evil actions. He hated Pedro, his brother, and he hated Claudio, because he was the prince's friend. He decided to prevent Claudio's marriage with Hero, only for the cruel pleasure of making Claudio and the prince unhappy, since he knew the prince was almost as eager for this marriage to take place as Claudio himself. To carry out this evil purpose, he employed Borachio, a man as bad as himself, whom he encouraged with the offer of a large reward. This Borachio was forming a relationship with Margaret, Hero's attendant. Knowing this, John persuaded him to make Margaret promise to talk to him from her lady's bedroom window that night, after Hero was asleep, and also to dress herself in Hero's clothes in order to make Claudio believe that she was Hero.

John then went to the prince and Claudio, and told them that Hero was the kind of woman who talked to men from her window at midnight. This was the evening before the wedding, and he offered to take them that night, so that they could hear Hero talking to a man. They agreed to go along with him, and Claudio said, 'If I see any reason tonight why I should not marry her, then I will shame her tomorrow in the church.' The prince also said, 'And as I helped you to win her, I will help you to shame her.'

When John brought them near Hero's room that night, they saw Borachio standing under the window, and they saw Margaret looking out of Hero's window, and heard her talking to Borachio. And since Margaret was dressed in the same clothes they had seen Hero wearing, the prince and Claudio believed it was the lady Hero herself.

Nothing could equal Claudio's anger, when he had made (as he thought) this discovery. All his love for sweet Hero was immediately turned into hatred, and he decided to shame her in the church the next day, as he had said he would. The prince agreed to this, thinking that no punishment could be too severe for a lady who talked to a man from her window the night before she was going to be married to Claudio.

◆

The next day they all met in church to celebrate the marriage. When Claudio and Hero were standing in front of the priest, and the priest was about to make them man and wife, Claudio angrily announced the guilt of the blameless Hero, who, shocked by his strange words, said quietly, 'Is my lord well, to speak in this way?'

Leonato, greatly shocked, said to the prince, 'My lord, why do you not speak?'

'What should I say?' said the prince. 'I stand dishonoured, since I have tried to join my dear friend to an unworthy woman. Leonato, on my honour, myself, my brother, and this poor Claudio here saw and heard her last night at midnight talking to a man at her window.'

Benedick, shocked at what he heard, said, 'It does not look as if there will be a marriage.'

'Oh, God!' replied Hero; and then this unhappy lady fainted and was, to all appearance, dead.

The prince and Claudio left the church without staying to see how Hero was or considering the sorrow into which they had thrown Leonato.

Benedick remained, while Beatrice tried to bring Hero out of her faint.

'How is the lady?' he asked.

'Dead, I think,' replied Beatrice in great grief; she loved her cousin and, knowing her goodness, believed nothing of what she had heard spoken against her.

Unlike the poor old father! He believed the story of his child's shame, and it was pitiful to hear him crying over her, as she lay in front of him, and wishing she would never again open her eyes.

But the old priest was a wise man, and knowledgable of human nature, and he had carefully noted the lady's face when she heard herself blamed. He said to the sorrowing father, 'Call me a fool if you like, and ignore my age and experience of men, but I have no doubt that this sweet lady is not guilty of these crimes.'

When Hero was herself again, the priest said to her, 'Lady, what man is it that they say you have been seeing?'

Hero replied, 'They know; I know of no one.' Then, turning to Leonato, she said, 'Oh, my father, if you can prove that any man has ever talked to me at unsuitable hours, or that last night I exchanged words with any creature, then hate me, punish me, kill me.'

'There is,' said the priest, 'some strange misunderstanding here.' He advised Leonato to report that Hero was dead; to dig a grave for her, and hold all the funeral ceremonies.

'What will the result be?' said Leonato. 'What good will this do?'

The priest replied, 'This report of her death will change evil thoughts into pity; that will do some good, but not all the good I hope for. When Claudio hears that she died after hearing his words, he will feel grief and wish that he had been gentler with her: yes, even though he thought what he said was true.'

33

Benedick now said, 'Leonato, take the priest's advice; and though you know how well I love the prince and Claudio, on my honour I will not tell them this secret.'

Leonato was persuaded and agreed. So the kind priest led him and Hero away to comfort them, and Beatrice and Benedick remained alone. And this was the meeting from which their friends, who had planned to bring them together, expected so much laughter; those friends who were now beaten down with grief, and from whose minds all thoughts of happiness seemed to have gone for ever.

Benedick was the first to speak, and he said, 'Lady Beatrice, have you been crying?'

'Yes, and I will cry for a while longer,' said Beatrice.

'Surely,' said Benedick, 'your fair cousin has been wronged.'

'Ah!' said Beatrice. 'I will owe so much to any man who helps her now!'

Benedick then said, 'Is there any way to show such friendship? I love nothing in the world as much as I do you; is that not strange?'

'It would be as possible,' said Beatrice, 'for me to say I loved nothing in the world as much as I do you; but at the moment I am sorry for my cousin and have no other feelings.'

'By my sword,' said Benedick, 'you love me, and I swear I love you. Come, tell me what I can do for you.'

'Kill Claudio,' said Beatrice.

'Not for the wide world!' said Benedick; for he loved Claudio, and he believed his friend had been deceived.

'Is Claudio not a bad man who has wronged and dishonoured my cousin?' said Beatrice. 'Oh, I wish I were a man!'

'Listen, Beatrice!' said Benedick.

But Beatrice would hear nothing in Claudio's defence; and she continued to urge Benedick to right her cousin's wrongs. She said, 'Talk to a man out of the window – a likely thing! Sweet

Hero! She has been wronged; she has lost everything. I wish I were a man for Claudio! Or that I had any friend who would be a man for me! But bravery melts into kind words. No amount of wishing will make me a man, so I will die from grief as a woman.'

'Wait, good Beatrice,' said Benedick. 'Do you truly believe that Claudio has wronged Hero?'

'Yes,' answered Beatrice. 'There is no doubt.'

'Enough,' said Benedick. 'I am satisfied; I will call him out and fight him. I will kiss your hand, and leave you. With this hand, Claudio shall pay for his deeds! Go, comfort your cousin.'

While Beatrice was urging Benedick into action to help Hero, by fighting with his dear friend Claudio, Leonato was calling on the prince and Claudio to answer with their swords for the injury they had done his child, who, he said, had died of grief. But they respected his age and his sorrow, and said, 'No, do not quarrel with us, good old man.' And now Benedick came, and he also called on Claudio to answer with his sword for the injury he had done to Hero, and Claudio and the prince said to each other, 'Beatrice has encouraged him to do this.'

But at this moment the justice of Heaven brought better proof that Hero was not guilty – certainly better proof than the uncertain fortune of a fight.

While the prince and Claudio were still talking about Benedick's threat, Borachio was brought as a prisoner in front of the prince. He had been overheard talking with one of his companions about the job he had been employed by John to do.

Borachio made a full statement to the prince in Claudio's hearing, swearing that it was Margaret, dressed in her lady's clothes, that he had talked to at the window, whom they had mistaken for the lady Hero herself. And so no doubt about Hero's goodness remained in the minds of Claudio and the prince. John, finding his evil was discovered, escaped from Messina to avoid the just anger of his brother.

Claudio's heart was full of grief when he found he had made false statements about Hero, who, he thought, had died on hearing his cruel words. The memory of Hero, the woman he loved, came over him; and he said that he felt as if he had taken poison while Borachio was speaking.

Claudio therefore asked forgiveness of the old man Leonato for the injury he had done his child, and promised that he would bear whatever punishment Leonato gave him for his fault in believing the false charge against the woman he had promised to marry.

The punishment which Leonato gave him was to marry the next morning a cousin of Hero's, who, he said, was now the person to whom he would leave his property, and who was in appearance very like Hero. Claudio, respecting the promise he had made to Leonato, said he would marry this unknown lady, regardless of how plain she might be. But his heart was very sad, and he spent that night in tears and bitter grief besides the stone cross which Leonato had built on Hero's grave.

When the morning came, the prince went with Claudio to the church. There the good priest, and Leonato and his niece, were already waiting to celebrate a second marriage. And Leonato presented to Claudio his new wife; but her face was covered so that Claudio could not see her. And Claudio said to the lady, 'Give me your hand in front of this priest; I am your husband if you will marry me.'

'And when I lived, I was your other wife,' said this unknown lady; and, uncovering her face, she proved to be no niece, but Leonato's daughter, Hero herself.

We may be sure that this proved a most pleasant surprise to Claudio, who thought that she was dead. He could hardly believe his eyes for joy. And the prince, who was equally surprised at what he saw, cried out, 'Is this not Hero, Hero that was dead?'

Leonato replied, 'She died, my lord, but only while the charge against her lived.'

The priest promised to explain everything when the service had ended, and he was about to marry them when he was interrupted by Benedick, who wanted to be married to Beatrice at the same time. Beatrice at first said no to this; but Benedick said she should admit her love for him, which he had learned about from Hero. So then a pleasant explanation took place, and they found they had both been tricked into believing the existence of a love which had never existed. But the love which a trick had sown had grown too powerful to be shaken. Benedick refused to consider anything that the world could say against his marriage; and he continued the joke, and swore to Beatrice that he was only taking her out of pity because he had heard she was dying of love for him. Beatrice on her side said that she was only giving way to great persuasion, and partly to save his life, since she had heard he was dangerously sick.

So these two crazy characters became friends and were married too, after Claudio and Hero were married. To finish the story, John was caught and brought back to Messina; and it was a fine punishment for this dark, unhappy man to see the joy and celebrations which, after the failure of his evil plans, took place at the palace in Messina.

As You Like It

A long time ago a certain part of France was ruled by a duke who had taken the position from his older brother, the lawful ruler. The true duke, who was driven away, went with a few trusted followers to the forest of Arden and lived there with his loving friends, who had gladly left home for him while their land and property made his brother rich. The carefree life they led here soon seemed sweeter to them than the grand life at court and many young men came daily to this forest from the court, and spent the time without cares, like those who lived in the golden age long, long ago. In the summer they lay under the fine shade of the large forest trees, watching the wild animals; and they became so fond of these poor creatures that they could not kill them for food. When the cold winds of winter made the duke feel that his fortune was changing, he would bear it, and say, 'These cold winds which blow on my body are true friends; they tell me my condition truly. And though their bite is sharp, it is nothing like as painful as that of the unkind and ungrateful.' In this manner the duke took a useful lesson from everything that he saw. He could find tongues in trees, books in the running streams, wise words in stones, and good in everything.

◆

The true duke had one daughter, named Rosalind, whom the unlawful Duke Frederick, when he drove out her father, still kept in his court as a companion for his own daughter, Celia. A close friendship had grown up between these ladies, which the quarrels of their fathers did not break. Celia tried by every kindness in her power to repay Rosalind for the injustice done to her and her father; and whenever the thoughts of her father's sorrow made Rosalind sad, Celia's only concern was to comfort and cheer her.

One day, when Celia was talking to Rosalind, a message came from the duke to tell them that if they wished to see a wrestling match, which was just about to begin, they must come immediately to the courtyard in front of the palace; and Celia, thinking it would amuse Rosalind, agreed to go and see it.

In those days wrestling was a favourite sport even in the courts of princes, and in front of fair ladies and princesses. When they arrived, Celia and Rosalind found that it was likely to end in tragedy, since a large and powerful man, who had years of experience in the art of wrestling and had killed many men in matches of this kind, was going to wrestle with a very young man, who, it seemed, would certainly be killed.

When the duke saw Celia and Rosalind, he said, 'Well, daughter and niece, have you come to see the wrestling? You will take little pleasure in it, as there is such a difference between the men. Out of pity for this young man, I would like to discourage him from wrestling. Speak to him, ladies, and see if you can persuade him.'

The ladies were very pleased to try. First Celia begged this young stranger not to attempt the fight; and then Rosalind spoke so kindly to him that instead of being persuaded by her gentle words to give up, he thought only of how he could prove his courage in this lovely lady's eyes. And he said: 'I am sorry to refuse such beautiful ladies anything. But let your fair eyes and gentle wishes go with me to the match. If I am killed, well, I am ready to die. I shall do my friends no wrong, for I have none to cry for me. I shall do the world no harm, for I have nothing in it. I only take up a place in the world which may be better filled when I have made it empty.'

◆

And now the wrestling match began. Celia hoped the young stranger would not be hurt, but Rosalind felt most for him. She thought that he was like herself, friendless and unfortunate; and she pitied him so much, and took so deep an interest in the danger he was in while he was wrestling, that she was almost in love with him already.

The kindness shown to this unknown youth by these ladies gave him courage and strength, so that he performed surprisingly well. In the end his opponent was defeated and so badly hurt that for a while he was unable to speak or move.

The Duke Frederick was very pleased with the courage and skill shown by this young stranger and asked about his name and family, intending to take him under his care.

The stranger said his name was Orlando, and that he was the youngest son of Sir Rowland de Boys.

Sir Rowland de Boys, Orlando's father, had been dead for some years; but when he was alive, he was a true subject and dear friend of the former duke. So, when Frederick heard that Orlando was the son of his brother's friend, all his liking for this brave young man was changed into dislike, and he walked away in anger. Hating to hear even the name of any of his brother's friends, but still admiring the courage of the youth, he said, as he left, that he wished Orlando were the son of any other man.

Rosalind was very pleased to hear that her new favourite was the son of her father's old friend. She and Celia then went up to him and, seeing him troubled by the duke's sudden anger, they spoke kind words to him. And when they were leaving him again, Rosalind turned back for a few more words with the brave young son of her father's old friend. Taking a chain from around her neck, she said, 'Sir, wear this for me. I wish I could give you a more valuable present.'

◆

When the ladies were alone, Rosalind's talk was still of Orlando, and Celia began to realize that her cousin had fallen in love with him. So she said to Rosalind, 'Is it possible you could fall in love so suddenly?'

Rosalind replied, 'The duke, my father, loved his father dearly.'

'But,' said Celia, 'does it therefore follow that you should love his son dearly? In that case I ought to hate him, since my father hated his father; but I do not hate Orlando.'

Frederick had been angry at the sight of Sir Rowland de Boys's son, which reminded him of the many friends his brother had. He had for some time been displeased with his niece, because people praised her for her goodness and pitied her for what had happened to her good father. So now he suddenly turned against her. While Celia and Rosalind were talking about Orlando, he came into the room and ordered Rosalind to leave the palace immediately and follow her father; he told Celia, who spoke for her without success, that he had only allowed Rosalind to stay because she wanted it.

'I did not ask you to let her stay,' said Celia, 'since I was too young at that time to value her; but now I know her worth. We have slept together for so long, risen at the same time, learned, played, and eaten together; I cannot live without her.'

Frederick replied, 'She is too clever for you; she makes people pity her. You are a fool to beg for her, as you will seem more attractive when she is gone. So do not open your lips in her support, for the judgement which I have passed on her cannot be changed.'

◆

When Celia found she could not persuade her father to let Rosalind remain with her, she decided to go with her and, leaving her father's palace that night, she went with her friend to find Rosalind's father, the true duke, in the forest of Arden.

Before they set out, Celia thought that it would be unsafe for two young ladies to travel in the rich clothes they usually wore; she therefore suggested that they should dress themselves like country girls. Rosalind said it would be even better if one of them dressed like a man; and so it was quickly agreed between them that Rosalind should wear the dress of a young man, and Celia that of a country girl, and that they should say they were brother and sister. Rosalind said she would be called Ganymede, and Celia chose the name of Aliena.

In this dress, then, these fair princesses set out on their long journey; for the forest of Arden was a long way away, beyond the borders of the duke's lands.

The lady Rosalind (or Ganymede as she must now be called) seemed to have developed a manly courage with her manly clothes. The friendship that Celia showed in walking with her for so many long miles made Rosalind put on a cheerful face, as if she were really Ganymede, the courageous brother of the gentle village girl, Aliena.

◆

When at last they came to the forest of Arden, they no longer found the comfortable accommodation that they had stayed in on the road, and they were soon in urgent need of food and rest. Ganymede, who had encouraged his sister with pleasant speeches and cheerful remarks all the way, now said he was so tired he could bring shame to his man's clothes, and cry like a woman, and Aliena too said she could go no further. Then Ganymede tried to remember that it was a man's duty to comfort a woman, so he said, 'Cheer up, my sister Aliena; we are now at the end of our journey, in the forest of Arden.' But such false courage would no longer help them; for though they were in the forest of Arden, they did not know where to find the duke. And here the journey of these tired ladies might have come to a sad end, since they might have got lost and died for lack of food. But happily, as they were sitting on the grass, nearly dead with tiredness, a countryman chanced to pass that way, and Ganymede once more tried to speak with a manly confidence, saying, 'Shepherd, will love or gold in this lonely place bring us food and shelter? I beg you to take us somewhere where we may rest; for this young woman, my sister, is tired from travelling, and faint for want of food.'

The man replied that he was only a servant to a shepherd, and that his master's house was going to be sold, and therefore they would find only poor accommodation; but that if they would go with him, they would be welcome. They followed the man, the thought of rest giving them fresh strength. Then they bought the house and sheep from the shepherd, and employed the man who had led them there to help them. Having now a pleasant house, and good food, they decided to stay there until they could learn which part of the forest the duke lived in.

When they felt better after their journey, they began to like their new way of life, and almost thought they were the shepherd and shepherdess they pretended to be. But sometimes Ganymede remembered he had once been the same lady Rosalind who had so dearly loved the brave Orlando because he was the son of her father's friend. And though Ganymede thought that Orlando was many miles distant, it soon happened that Orlando was also in the forest of Arden, and a strange event took place.

◆

Orlando was the youngest son of Sir Rowland de Boys, who, when he died, left him in the care of his oldest brother Oliver. Oliver was told to give Orlando a good education, and to provide for him in a manner worthy of their ancient family. Oliver, though, never sent his brother to school, and kept him at home untaught. But in his nature Orlando was so much like his father that even without any good education he seemed well educated. Oliver hated him so much that in the end he decided to kill him; and for that reason he sent him to wrestle with the famous wrestler who had killed so many men. It was this cruel brother's behaviour towards him which made Orlando say he wished to die because he was so friendless.

When Orlando defeated the wrestler instead of being killed by him, Oliver swore he would set fire to the room where Orlando slept. A man who had been an old and trusted servant to their father, and who loved Orlando because he was like Sir Rowland, heard him saying this. This old man went out to meet Orlando when he returned from the palace, and when he saw his young master, the danger he was in made him cry out, 'O my sweet master! Why are you so good? Why are you gentle, strong, and brave? And how did you manage to defeat the famous wrestler? News of your success has arrived home too quickly before you.'

Orlando, confused as to what all this meant, asked him what the matter was. And then the old man told him how his evil brother, hearing of the fame he had won by his victory at the

duke's palace, intended to kill him by setting fire to his room that
night; and he warned the young man to leave immediately.
Knowing Orlando had no money, Adam (for that was the old
man's name) had brought out with him his own little bag of
savings, and he said, 'I have five hundred pounds, saved when
your father was alive to support me when my old legs become
unfit for service; take that, and may God who feeds the birds give
me comfort in my old age! Here is the gold; all this is for you.
But let me be your servant even though I look old.'

'Oh, good old man!' said Orlando. 'How well the trusted
service of the old world is shown in you! You do not belong in
these times. We will travel together, and before your savings are
spent I shall find some way to support us both.'

Together, then, this old servant and his master set out; and
Orlando and Adam travelled on, uncertain which way to go, until
they came to the forest of Arden. There they found themselves in
the same pain for lack of food as Ganymede and Aliena. They
wandered on until they were almost dead with hunger and
tiredness. Adam at last said, 'Oh, my dear master, I can go no
further!' He lay down, thinking he would make that place his
grave, and said goodbye to his master. Orlando, seeing him in this
weak state, took his old servant in his arms, and carried him to
the shelter of some pleasant trees. Then he said to him, 'Do not
give up, old Adam; rest your tired legs here for a while, and do
not talk of dying.'

Orlando then searched around to find some food, and he
arrived by chance in that part of the forest where the duke was.
The duke and his friends were just going to eat their dinner,
seated on the grass under the shade of some large trees.

Orlando, whom hunger had made half crazy, pulled out his
sword, intending to take their food by force, and said, 'Eat no
more; I must have your food!' The duke asked him if misfortune
had made him so violent, or if he were a rough man who knew

nothing of good manners. So then Orlando said he was dying of hunger, and the duke told him he was welcome to sit down and eat with them. Orlando, hearing him speak so gently, put away his sword, and turned red with shame at the rude manner in which he had spoken.

'Pardon me, I beg you,' said he. 'I thought that everything would be wild here, and so I put on this hard, commanding expression. But whoever you are, if you have ever seen better days; if you have ever been to a place where church bells ring; if you have ever sat at any good man's table; if tears have ever fallen from your eyes, and if you have known what it is to pity or be pitied, may gentle speeches now move you to be kind to me!'

The duke replied, 'It is true that we are men (as you say) who have seen better days. Though we now live in this wild forest, we have lived in towns and cities where church bells ring, have sat at good men's tables, and have cried tears of pity. So sit down and take as much of our food as you need.'

'There is a poor old man,' answered Orlando, 'who has walked behind me for mile after mile from pure love, and is now suffering from both age and hunger; until he is satisfied, I can touch nothing.'

'Go and bring him here,' said the duke. 'We will not eat until you return.' Then Orlando ran to find Adam, and soon returned with him in his arms. The duke said, 'Set him down; you are both welcome.' And they fed the old man, and cheered his heart, and he regained his health and strength.

The duke asked who Orlando was; and when he found that he was the son of his old friend, Sir Rowland de Boys, he took him under his care, and Orlando and his old servant lived with the duke in the forest.

All this happened not many days after Ganymede and Aliena came to the forest and (as has already been told) bought the shepherd's home.

♦

Ganymede and Aliena were very surprised to find the name of Rosalind cut into the trees, and love poems tied to them, all addressed to Rosalind. While they were wondering how this could be, they met Orlando, and they saw the chain which Rosalind had given him around his neck.

Orlando did not know that Ganymede was the fair princess Rosalind who, by her kindness, had so won his heart that he spent his whole time cutting her name into the trees, and writing poems in praise of her beauty. But he liked the look of this shepherd-boy, and began to talk to him. He thought he saw a similarity between Ganymede and his Rosalind, but noted that he had none of the fine manners of that lady, since Ganymede put on the manners often seen in young men. With much laughter Ganymede talked to Orlando about a certain lover, 'who,' said he, 'lives in our forests, and spoils our young trees by cutting "Rosalind" into them; and he hangs poems on the bushes, all praising this same Rosalind. If I could find this lover, I would give him some good advice that would soon cure him of his love.'

Orlando said that he was the foolish lover of whom he spoke, and asked Ganymede to give him the good advice he had mentioned. The cure Ganymede offered, and the advice he gave him, was that Orlando should come every day to the small house where he and his sister Aliena lived. 'And then,' said Ganymede, 'I will pretend that I am Rosalind, and you will pretend to make love to me just as you would do if I were Rosalind. And then I will copy the strange ways of ladies to their lovers, until I make you ashamed of your love; and this is the way I plan to cure you.'

Orlando did not think much of the cure, but he agreed to come every day to Ganymede's house and to do as he said. And every day Orlando visited Ganymede and Aliena, and Orlando called Ganymede his Rosalind and used the fine words with which young men please their ladies. But it did not appear that Ganymede made any progress in curing Orlando of his love for Rosalind.

Though Orlando thought all this was only a game (not dreaming that Ganymede was his own true Rosalind), it pleased him almost as much as it did Ganymede, who was secretly happy that these fine love speeches were all being spoken to the right person.

In this way many days passed pleasantly, and the good-natured Aliena, seeing that it made Ganymede happy, let him have his own way and did not remind him that the lady Rosalind had not yet made herself known to the duke, her father. Ganymede met the duke one day, and talked to him, and the duke asked what family he came from. Ganymede answered that he came from as good a family as he did. This made the duke smile, since he did not think the pretty shepherd-boy was of royal blood. Since the duke looked well and happy, Ganymede decided to keep his secret a few days more.

◆

One morning as Orlando was going to see Ganymede, he saw a man lying asleep on the ground with a large green snake twisted around his neck. The snake noticed Orlando and moved quietly away through the bushes. Orlando went nearer, and then he found a lioness lying with her head on the ground, waiting for the sleeping man to wake (for it is said that lions will seize nothing that is dead or sleeping). It seemed as if Orlando had been sent by God to free the man from the danger of the snake and the lioness. When Orlando looked into the man's face, he saw that the sleeper was his own brother Oliver, who had used him so cruelly, and he was almost tempted to leave him to be eaten by the hungry lioness. Brotherly love was stronger, though, than his anger against his brother. He pulled out his sword, and attacked the lioness, and killed her, and so he saved his brother's life both from the poisonous snake and from the lioness; but before Orlando could kill her, the lioness managed to tear one of his arms.

While Orlando was fighting with the lioness, Oliver awoke and saw that his brother Orlando, whom he had treated so cruelly, was saving him from a wild animal at the risk of his own life. Shame and guilt seized him, and he begged his brother's pardon for the wrong he had done him. Orlando was glad to see him so sorry, and forgave him immediately. They kissed each other, and from that hour Oliver loved Orlando with a true brotherly love, though he had come to the forest to kill him.

The wound in Orlando's arm bled so much that he found himself too weak to go to visit Ganymede, and therefore he asked his brother to go and tell Ganymede about his accident.

So Oliver went, and told Ganymede and Aliena how Orlando had saved his life. When he had finished the story of Orlando's bravery, and his own escape, he admitted to them that he was Orlando's cruel brother, and then he told them of their new-found love.

The true sorrow that Oliver showed when he spoke of his offences had such a powerful effect on Aliena's kind heart that she immediately fell in love with him; and Oliver, seeing how much she pitied him, fell in love just as suddenly with her. But Ganymede fainted at the news that Orlando had been in danger, and that he had been wounded by the lioness. When he became conscious again, he told Oliver that he had only pretended to faint, but Oliver saw by the paleness of his face that he had really fainted and he was much surprised at the weakness of the young man.

Oliver made his visit a very long one, and when at last he returned to his brother, he had a great deal of news to tell him.

He told him about Ganymede fainting when he heard that Orlando was wounded, and of how he had fallen in love with the fair shepherdess Aliena, and that she had listened to him kindly even at this first meeting. And he said to his brother, as if it were almost definite, that he would marry Aliena. He loved her so well, he said, that he would live there as a shepherd and give his lands and house to Orlando.

'Well,' said Orlando, 'let your wedding be tomorrow, and I will invite the duke and his friends. Go and ask your shepherdess to agree to this; she is now alone – look, here comes her brother.' Oliver went to see Aliena; and Ganymede, whom Orlando had seen coming, came to ask after the health of his wounded friend.

When Orlando and Ganymede began to discuss the sudden love between Oliver and Aliena, Orlando said he had advised his brother to ask his fair shepherdess to marry him the next day, and then he added how much he wished he could be married on the same day to his Rosalind.

Ganymede said that if Orlando really loved Rosalind as much as he said he did, he would have his wish. For on the next day he would make sure Rosalind herself appeared, and he knew that Rosalind would agree to marry Orlando.

This, he said, he would arrange with the help of magic which he had learnt from an uncle who was a famous magician.

The hopeful lover Orlando, half believing and half doubting what he heard, asked Ganymede if he could really do this. 'By my life I can,' said Ganymede, 'so put on your best clothes, and call the duke and your friends to your wedding; for if you wish to be married tomorrow to Rosalind, she will be here.'

The next morning, Oliver and Aliena came into the presence of the duke, and Orlando came with them.

When they had all come together for this double marriage, there was much wondering, since only one of the young women had appeared, but most people thought that Ganymede was making fun of Orlando.

The duke, hearing that it was his own daughter who was to be brought there in this strange way, asked Orlando if he believed the shepherd-boy could really do what he had promised. And while Orlando was answering that he did not know what to think, Ganymede entered and asked the duke whether he would agree to his daughter's marriage with Orlando.

'I would,' said the duke, 'if I had lands to give with her.'

Ganymede then said to Orlando, 'And you say you will marry her if I bring her here.'

'I would,' said Orlando, 'if I were king of many lands.'

Ganymede and Aliena then went out together, and Ganymede threw off his man's clothes, dressed again as a woman, and quickly became Rosalind without the power of magic; and Aliena, putting on her own rich clothes, was with just as little difficulty changed into the lady Celia.

While they were gone, the duke said to Orlando that he thought the shepherd Ganymede was very like his daughter Rosalind; and Orlando said that he thought so too.

They had no time to wonder how all this would end, since Rosalind and Celia entered in their own clothes; and, no longer pretending that it was by the power of magic that she came there, Rosalind threw herself on her knees in front of her father and kissed his hand. The moment seemed so surprising to everyone present that it might well have passed for magic, but Rosalind told him how she had left the palace and lived in the forest as a shepherd-boy with her cousin Celia as her sister.

The duke agreed to the marriage, and Orlando and Rosalind, Oliver and Celia were married at the same time. And though their wedding could not be celebrated in grand style in this wild forest, there never has been a happier wedding day; and while they were eating under the cool shade of the pleasant trees, a messenger arrived to tell the duke the joyful news that his property and rightful position had been returned to him.

◆

Frederick, angry at the flight of his daughter Celia, had put himself at the head of a large army and ridden towards the forest, intending to seize his brother with all his followers and kill him. But just as he entered the wild forest, he was met by an old religious man, with whom he had a long conversation, and who in the end completely changed his mind about his evil plan. He became truly sorry, and decided to return what he had stolen from his brother and to spend the rest of his days with religious men. His first act was to send a messenger to his brother (as has been told), to give him back his title, and with it the property and income of his friends and followers.

This happy news came just in time to crown the joy of all who were at the wedding of the princesses. Celia was sincerely pleased at her cousin's good fortune, though Rosalind, not she, would now be rich.

The duke at last had the opportunity to reward those true friends who had stayed with him in the forest; and these worthy followers, though they had patiently shared his troubles, were very well pleased to return in peace and wealth to the palace of their lawful duke.

The Merchant of Venice

CHARACTERS
The Duke of Venice
Antonio, a young merchant of Venice
Bassanio, his friend
Gratiano, a gentleman attending Bassanio
Shylock, the moneylender
Portia, a lady living at Belmont
Nerissa, Portia's servant

Shylock, a Jew, lived in Venice. He had made himself very rich by lending money at great interest to Christian merchants. Being a hard-hearted man, he used such cruelty to force people to repay the money he had lent them that he was much hated by all good men, and particularly by Antonio, a young merchant of Venice. And Shylock hated Antonio just as much, because Antonio also lent money to people who were in trouble, but he would never take any interest for the money he lent. Whenever Antonio met Shylock, he complained about his hard business dealings; and Shylock would bear these complaints with seeming patience, while secretly planning to hurt him.

Antonio was the kindest man that lived. He was greatly loved by all those who knew him, but the friend who was nearest and dearest to his heart was Bassanio, a high-ranking Venetian who had wasted his small fortune by living in too expensive a manner (as young men of high rank with small fortunes often do). Whenever Bassanio wanted money, Antonio helped him.

One day Bassanio came to Antonio and told him that he wished to make a wealthy marriage with a lady whom he dearly loved. Her father, who had recently died, had left her a large property. In her father's lifetime (he said) he used to visit her house, and sometimes he thought he could read silent messages in this lady's eyes; but he did not have enough money to make himself appear the lover of so rich a lady, so he begged Antonio to lend him three thousand pounds.

Antonio had no money at the time to lend his friend; but, expecting to have some ships come home soon with goods for sale, he said he would go to Shylock, the rich moneylender, and borrow the money for his friend.

Antonio and Bassanio went together to Shylock, and Antonio asked the Jew to lend him three thousand pounds at any interest he wished, to be paid out of the goods in his ships at sea.

Shylock thought to himself, 'If I can catch him once, I will punish him. He hates our Jewish nation; he lends out money without interest; and among the merchants, he speaks badly of me and my good business.'

Antonio, seeing he was thinking and did not answer, and being anxious to get the money, said, 'Shylock, do you hear me? Will you lend the money?'

To this question Shylock replied, 'Signor Antonio, many a time you have complained about me, and I have borne your rudeness patiently; and you have called me an unbeliever, and kicked at me with your foot as if I were a dog. Well, it now appears that you need my help. So you come to me and say, "Shylock, lend me money". Does a dog have money? Is it possible a dog could lend three thousand pounds? Shall I show you respect and say, "Sir, you swore at me last Wednesday, and another time you called me dog; for these kind deeds, should I lend you money?"'

Antonio replied, 'I am as likely to call you names again, and kick you too. If you will lend me this money, do not lend it as you would to a friend, but lend it as you would to an enemy, so that if I cannot repay you, you can punish me more easily.'

'Well, there is no need to shout!' said Shylock. 'I would be glad to be friends with you, and forget how you have shamed me. I will supply your wants, and take no interest for my money.' This offer greatly surprised Antonio; but then Shylock, still pretending to be kind, repeated that he would lend him three thousand pounds and take no interest for his money. The only condition was that Antonio should go with him to a lawyer and sign a paper agreeing that if he did not repay the money by a certain day, he would lose a pound of flesh, to be cut off from any part of his body that Shylock pleased.

'Don't worry,' said Antonio, 'I will sign this paper, and say there is much kindness in the Jew.'

Bassanio said Antonio should not sign such a paper for him; but still Antonio said that he would sign it, since before the day of payment came, his ships would come back with many times the value of the money.

Shylock, hearing this talk, cried out, 'Oh, what evil these Christians find in others! Tell me this, Bassanio: if he should break his word, what would I gain? A pound of flesh, taken from a man, is not worth so much as the flesh of a lamb or a cow. I am offering this money in friendship: if he wants it, he can take it; if not, goodbye.'

At last, against the advice of Bassanio, Antonio signed the paper, thinking it really was just a joke.

◆

The rich lady that Bassanio wished to marry lived near Venice, in a place called Belmont. Her name was Portia, and in the beauty of her person and her mind she was the equal of any woman that has ever lived.

Bassanio, having been so kindly supplied with money by his friend Antonio at the risk of his life, set out for Belmont with a large company of servants, and attended by a gentleman of the name of Gratiano.

Bassanio was successful, and Portia soon agreed to accept him as her husband.

Bassanio told Portia that he had little money, and that his high birth and family were all that he could speak proudly of; but she loved him for himself and had enough riches not to need a wealthy husband. She answered that she wished she were a thousand times more beautiful, and ten thousand times richer, so that she would be more worthy of him; and she told him she was just a silly girl, but not too old to learn, and that she would allow her gentle spirit to be directed and governed by him in all things. And she said, 'I now give you myself and everything I have. Only yesterday, Bassanio, I was the lady of this fair house, queen of myself and of these servants; and now this house, these servants and myself are yours, my lord – I give them with this ring.' She presented a ring to Bassanio.

Bassanio was so surprised and grateful at the way in which the rich and well-born Portia treated a poor man like him that he could only speak a few broken words of love; taking the ring, he swore never to part with it.

Gratiano and Nerissa, Portia's servant, were with their lord and lady when Portia so gracefully promised to become Bassanio's obedient wife; and Gratiano, wishing Bassanio and the lady joy, asked permission to be married at the same time.

'With all my heart, Gratiano,' said Bassanio, 'if you can get a wife.'

Gratiano then said that he loved the lady Portia's fair servant, Nerissa, and that she had promised to be his wife if her lady married Bassanio. Portia asked Nerissa if this was true. Nerissa replied, 'Madam, it is true, if you approve of it.' Portia gladly agreed to this, so Bassanio said pleasantly, 'Then our wedding party shall be much honoured by your marriage, Gratiano.'

◆

The happiness of these lovers was sadly destroyed at this moment by the entrance of a messenger, who brought a letter from Antonio containing terrible news. When Bassanio read Antonio's letter, he looked so pale that Portia feared it was to tell him of the death of some dear friend. She asked what the news was which had upset him so much, and he said, 'Oh, sweet Portia, here are some of the most unpleasant words that were ever written. Gentle lady, when I first spoke to you of my love, I admitted that all the wealth I had was my high-born blood; but I should have told you that I had less than nothing, since I am in debt.' Bassanio then told Portia about how he had borrowed money from Antonio, and about Antonio borrowing it from Shylock, and about the legal agreement by which Antonio had promised to give a pound of flesh if the money were not paid back by a certain day. And then Bassanio read Antonio's letter to her; the words of which were:

Dear Bassanio,

My ships are all lost, I must pay Shylock, and since I cannot both pay and live, I would like to see you at my death. But do as you please; if your love for me does not make you come, do not let my letter influence you.

'Oh, my dear love,' said Portia, 'finish your business and be gone. You shall have gold to pay the money back 20 times over before this kind friend loses even a hair for helping you.'

Portia then said she wanted to be married to Bassanio before he left, to give him a legal right to her money. So that same day they were married, and Gratiano was also married to Nerissa; and Bassanio and Gratiano, as soon as they were married, set out at great speed for Venice, where Bassanio found Antonio in prison.

Since the day of payment had passed, cruel Shylock would not accept the money which Bassanio offered him, but said he must have a pound of Antonio's flesh. A day was fixed for the Duke of Venice to hear the case, and Bassanio waited with a troubled mind.

◆

When Portia's husband left, she spoke encouragingly to him and told him to bring his dear friend back with him when he returned. But she feared it would not be so easy to save Antonio, and when she was left alone she began to wonder if she could save the life of her dear Bassanio's friend herself. And though she had said in such a gentle and wifelike way that she would be ruled in all things by his wisdom, she quickly decided to go to Venice and speak in Antonio's defence.

Portia had a relation who was a lawyer. She wrote to this gentleman, whose name was Bellario, asking him to advise her and to lend her lawyer's clothes. When the messenger returned, he brought letters of advice from Bellario and also everything necessary for her journey.

Portia dressed herself and her servant Nerissa in men's clothes; she wore the clothes of a lawyer and she took Nerissa along with her as her clerk. Then, leaving immediately, they arrived at Venice on the day that the case was to be heard in the courthouse in front of the Duke of Venice. Portia entered and handed the duke a letter from Bellario to say that he would have come himself to speak for Antonio, but that he was sick and could not, and to ask if the learned young Doctor Balthasar (so he called Portia) could speak instead of him. The duke agreed to this, rather surprised by the youthful face of the stranger, whose true appearance was hidden by her lawyer's dress.

And now this important case began. Portia looked around her and saw the hard-hearted Shylock; and she saw Bassanio, but he did not know her in her lawyer's clothes. He was standing beside Antonio, in a state of very great anxiety and fear for his friend.

◆

Portia began by addressing herself to Shylock. He had a right (she said) by Venetian law to have what was promised in the agreement; but she spoke so sweetly of the quality of mercy that any heart except the unfeeling Shylock's would have softened. She said that mercy dropped like the gentle rain from heaven on the place beneath; that it was a quality of God himself and so a finer thing for a king than his crown. 'Remember,' she said, 'that as we all pray for mercy, that same prayer should teach us to show mercy.'

Shylock only answered her by demanding what the contract promised. 'Is he not able to pay the money?' asked Portia. Bassanio then said he would pay the three thousand pounds as many times over as Shylock wished; but the moneylender refused, and still said he must have a pound of Antonio's flesh. So Bassanio begged the learned young lawyer to try and bend the law a little, to save Antonio's life. But Portia answered that once laws had been passed they could not be changed in that way. Shylock heard Portia say that the law could not be changed, and thought that she was supporting his case, and he said, 'Oh, wise young judge, how I honour you! You are so much older than your looks!'

Portia now asked Shylock to let her look at the contract; and when she had read it, she said, 'By this contract this man may lawfully claim a pound of flesh, to be cut off by him from a place near Antonio's heart.' Then she said to Shylock, 'Be merciful; take the money, and tell me to tear up the paper.'

But the cruel Shylock would show no mercy, and he said, 'By my soul, I swear that there is no power in a man's tongue to change my mind.'

'Well, then, Antonio,' said Portia, 'you must prepare your breast for the knife.' And while Shylock was sharpening a long knife, with great eagerness, to cut off the pound of flesh, Portia asked Antonio, 'Have you anything to say?'

Antonio replied in a calm voice that he had little to say, as he had prepared his mind for death. Then he said to Bassanio, 'Give me your hand, Bassanio! Goodbye! Do not be upset that you are the cause of this misfortune. Remember me to your honourable wife, and tell her how I have loved you!'

Bassanio replied sadly, 'Antonio, I am married to a wife who is as dear to me as life itself: but I do not value life itself, my wife, and all the world above your life. I would lose everything, I would give everything to this devil here to save you.'

When Portia heard this, she could not help answering, 'Your wife would not thank you, if she were present, to hear you make this offer.'

And then Gratiano, who loved to copy what his lord did, said, in Nerissa's hearing, 'I have a wife whom I love; I would wish her in heaven, if she could just beg some power there to change this cruel man's mind.'

'It is just as well you wish this behind her back, or you would have trouble in your house,' said Nerissa.

◆

Shylock cried out, 'We are wasting time; it is time to carry out the sentence.' And now every heart was full of grief for Antonio.

Portia said to the moneylender, 'Shylock, you must have some doctor here, in case he bleeds to death.'

Shylock, whose hope it was that Antonio would bleed to death, said, 'It does not say so in the contract.'

Portia replied, 'It does not say so in the contract, but what does that matter? It would be good if you did this out of kindness.'

To this the only answer Shylock would make was, 'I cannot find it in the contract.'

'Then,' said Portia, 'a pound of Antonio's flesh is yours. The law allows it, and the court gives it. And you may cut this flesh from his chest. The law allows it and the court gives it.'

Again Shylock cried out, 'Oh, wise and honest judge!'

And then he sharpened his long knife again and, looking eagerly at Antonio, said, 'Prepare yourself!'

'Wait,' said Portia; 'there is something else. This contract here gives you no drop of blood; the words are: "a pound of flesh". If, when the pound of flesh is cut off, one drop of blood falls, your land and goods will be taken from you by law and given to the state of Venice.'

Now it was quite impossible for Shylock to cut off the pound of flesh without some of Antonio's blood falling; so these wise words of Portia's, that it was flesh and not blood that was named in the contract, saved Antonio's life. And everyone admired the wisdom of the young lawyer and praised his skill in every part of the courthouse; and Gratiano said, in the words which Shylock had used, 'Oh, wise and honest judge!'

Shylock, finding himself beaten, said with a disappointed look that he would take the money; and Bassanio happily cried out, 'Here is the money!'

But Portia stopped him, saying, 'Wait; there is no hurry. This man shall have nothing except what is in the contract. Therefore get ready, Shylock, to cut off the flesh; but make sure that no blood falls, and do not cut off more or less than a pound. If you cut even the weight of a single hair over one pound, you will die by the laws of Venice, and all your wealth will become the state's.'

'Give me my money, and let me go,' said Shylock.

'I have it ready,' said Bassanio, 'here it is.'

Shylock was going to take the money when Portia stopped him again, saying, 'Wait, there is one more problem. By the laws of Venice, your wealth will go to the state, for having planned to kill one of its citizens; your life lies at the mercy of the duke, so get down on your knees and ask him to pardon you.'

◆

The duke then said to Shylock, 'So that you can see the difference between our ways and yours, I will give you your life before you ask for it. Half your wealth belongs to Antonio; the other half comes to the state.'

The generous Antonio then said that he would give up his share of Shylock's wealth, if Shylock would sign a contract to give it on his death to his daughter and her husband. (For Antonio knew that Shylock had an only daughter, who had recently married without his permission a young man called Lorenzo, a friend of Antonio's, which had made Shylock very angry with her.)

The Jew agreed to this and very unhappily said, 'I am ill. Let me go home; send the contract after me, and I will sign over half my riches to my daughter.'

'Go, then,' said the duke, 'and sign it; and if you are truly sorry for your cruelty, the state will forgive you the payment of the other half of your riches.'

The duke now set Antonio free, and left the court with his councillors; and then Bassanio said to Portia, 'Most worthy gentleman, my friend Antonio and I have been saved today by your wisdom, and I beg you to accept the three thousand pounds I was to pay Shylock.'

Portia would not accept the money; but when Bassanio still pressed her to accept a reward, she said, 'Give me your gloves, then; I will wear them.' And then, when Bassanio took off his gloves, she saw the ring which she had given him on his finger, and she said, 'And since you wish to reward me, I will take this ring from you.'

Bassanio was very upset that the lawyer asked him for the only thing he could not give, and he replied that he could not give him that ring, because it was a gift from his wife and he had promised never to part with it. But he added that he would give him the most expensive ring in Venice instead of that one. Portia pretended to be angry when she heard this, and left the court saying, 'I am not a beggar, but you are speaking as if I were one.'

'Dear Bassanio,' said Antonio, 'let him have the ring.'

Bassanio, ashamed to appear so ungrateful, sent Gratiano after Portia with the ring. And then the clerk Nerissa, who had also given Gratiano a ring, begged for his, and Gratiano (though he did not want to) gave it to her. And the two ladies laughed thinking about how they would punish their husbands for giving away their rings, and how they would pretend to believe that the men had given them as a present to some woman.

On the journey home, Portia was in that happy state of mind which comes from a good deed. She enjoyed everything she saw: the moon seemed to shine more brightly than ever before, and when that pleasant moon was hidden behind a cloud, then a light which she saw from her house in Belmont pleased her, and she said, 'That light we see is burning in my hall; just as that little lamp throws its beams so far, a good deed shines brightly in a bad world.' And hearing the sound of music from her house, she said, 'By night, music sounds much sweeter than by day.'

◆

And now Portia and Nerissa entered the house and, dressing themselves in their own clothes, waited for their husbands, who soon followed them with Antonio. Soon Nerissa and her husband began to quarrel in a corner of the room.

'A quarrel already?' said Portia. 'What is the matter?'

Gratiano replied, 'Lady, it is about a poor little ring that Nerissa gave me.'

'What does the value of the ring matter?' said Nerissa. 'You swore to me, when I gave it to you, that you would keep it until the hour of your death; and now you say you gave it to the lawyer's clerk. I know you gave it to a woman.'

'I promise,' replied Gratiano, 'I gave it to a boy no taller than yourself. He was a clerk to the young lawyer who by his wise words saved Antonio's life. This little boy begged for it as payment, and I could not say no to him.'

Portia said, 'You were to blame, Gratiano, to give away your wife's first gift. I gave my lord Bassanio a ring, and I am sure he would not part with it for all the world.'

Gratiano, to excuse his own fault, now said, 'My lord Bassanio gave his ring away to the lawyer, and then the boy, his clerk, begged for my ring.'

Portia, hearing this, seemed very angry, and blamed Bassanio for giving away her ring; she said that Nerissa had taught her what to believe, and that she knew some woman had the ring.

Bassanio was very unhappy to have made his dear wife angry, and he said, 'No, by my honour, no woman has it – only a lawyer who refused three thousand pounds from me and begged for the ring. What could I do, sweet Portia? I was so ashamed that I was forced to send the ring after him. Forgive me, good lady; if you had been there, I think you would have begged the ring from me to give to the good lawyer.'

'Ah!' said Antonio. 'I am the unhappy cause of these quarrels.'

Portia asked Antonio not to be upset about that; and then Antonio said, 'I once lent my body for Bassanio, and if it were not for the man to whom your husband gave the ring, I would now be dead. I can promise you that your lord will never again break your trust in him.'

'Then,' said Portia, 'give him this ring, and tell him to keep it safer than the other.'

When Bassanio looked at this ring, he was very surprised to

find it was the same as the one he had given away. And then Portia told him that she was the young lawyer, and Nerissa was her clerk. And Bassanio found, to his great wonder and joy, that it was through the courage and wisdom of his wife that Antonio's life had been saved.

And Portia welcomed Antonio again, and gave him letters in which there was an account of how Antonio's ships, that were said to have been lost, had arrived safely in the port. So the sad beginnings of this rich merchant's story were all forgotten in the good fortune which came later, and there was time to laugh at the strange story of the rings, and the husbands that did not recognize their own wives. Gratiano gladly swore that while he lived he would fear nothing so much as losing Nerissa's ring again.

Macbeth

At the time when Duncan ruled as King of Scotland, there lived a great lord called Macbeth. Macbeth was a close relative of the king, and was greatly respected at court for his courage in war.

The two Scottish generals, Macbeth and Banquo, were returning victorious from a great battle, when they were stopped by three strange figures. These figures were like women except that they had beards, and their lined skin and wild dress made them look unlike any earthly creatures. Macbeth addressed them first, but each one laid a finger on her thin lips as a signal that he should be silent, and the first of them called Macbeth by the title of Lord of Glamis. The general was much surprised to find himself known by such creatures; but he was even more shocked when the second of them gave him the title of Lord of Cawdor, to which honour he had no claim! And then the third called to him, 'Greetings to a future king!' Such words certainly surprised him, since he knew that while the king's sons lived he could not hope to become king. Then, turning to Banquo, they pronounced him to be both less than Macbeth and greater, not so happy, but much happier; they said that although he would never be king, his sons would be kings in Scotland. They then disappeared, and now the generals knew them to be witches.

While they stood thinking about these strange things, messengers arrived from the king, sent by him to give Macbeth the name and title of Cawdor. Macbeth was so surprised that the witches' words seemed to be coming true that he was unable to reply to the messengers. And at that moment the hope formed in his mind that what the third witch had said might also come true, and that he would one day be King of Scotland.

He said to Banquo, 'Do you not hope that your children will be kings, when what the witches promised to me has so surprisingly happened?'

'That hope,' answered Banquo, 'might make you plan to be king; often these ministers of darkness tell us small truths to lead us into evil deeds.'

But the words of the witches had sunk too deep into Macbeth's mind to allow him to listen to the warnings of the good Banquo. From that time he directed all his thoughts towards becoming King of Scotland.

◆

Macbeth had a wife, to whom he told the strange words of the witches, and what had followed. She was a bad woman, whose only desire was that her husband and herself should arrive at greatness by any means necessary. She never failed to remind Macbeth that the murder of the king was necessary for the words of the witches to come true.

It happened at this time that the king came to Macbeth's house with his two sons, Malcolm and Donalbain, and a large number of lords and attendants, to honour Macbeth for his success in the wars.

The castle of Macbeth was built in a beautiful spot. The king entered, well pleased with the place, and even more pleased with the attentions and respect of his honoured hostess, Lady Macbeth. She was able to hide evil purposes behind smiles, and could look like a beautiful flower while she was really the snake beneath it.

The king, who was tired after his journey, went to bed early, and two servants (as was the custom) slept beside him. He had been unusually pleased with his welcome, and had given presents to many of his officers; he had also sent a beautiful diamond to Lady Macbeth, his kind hostess.

◆

It was now the middle of night, when bad dreams trouble men's minds, and only the wild animal and the murderer are about. This was the time when Lady Macbeth woke to plan the murder of the king. She would not have decided to do something so unnatural to a woman herself if she did not fear her husband's nature – that it was too kind to plan a murder. She knew that he wanted to become king but also that he was not yet ready for that level of crime. She had persuaded him to agree to the murder, but she doubted his firmness, and she feared that the natural gentleness of his heart (more gentle than her own) would return and defeat the purpose. So with a knife in her own hands, she went to the king's bed, having taken care to make his servants drunk and unable to do their job. There lay Duncan, in a deep sleep; but as she looked closely at him, there was something in his sleeping face which made her think of her own father, and she did not have the heart to go on.

She returned to speak with her husband, who now considered that there were strong arguments against the deed. In the first place, he was not only a subject, but a near relative of the king; he had been his host that day, and it was a host's duty to shut the door against his murderers, not to use the knife himself. Then he thought how just and merciful a king this Duncan had been, how kind to his subjects, how loving towards others, and in particular to him; that such kings are the special care of Heaven, so their subjects had a double duty to punish those that hurt them. Besides, because the king trusted and liked him, Macbeth stood high in the opinion of all sorts of men, and this respect would be damaged by association with such a terrible murder!

So Lady Macbeth found her husband, after this inner struggle, deciding to go no further with the plan. But she was a woman who was not easily shaken from her evil purpose. She began to pour into his ears words which breathed some of her own spirit into his mind. She gave him many reasons why he should not turn from what he had promised: how easy the deed was; how soon it would be over; and how the action of one short night would give royal power to all their future nights and days! Then she added how easy it would be to blame the murder on the drunken, sleepy servants. And with the courage of her tongue she persuaded him that he should find the strength to do the bloody business.

So, taking the knife, he went quietly to where Duncan lay; but as he went, he thought he saw another knife in the air, with the handle towards him, and on the blade and at its point were drops of blood. And when he tried to take the knife, it was nothing but air, a dream that stemmed from his troubled brain and the business he was about to complete.

Driving away this fear, Macbeth entered the king's room and killed him with one stroke of his knife. One of the servants in the room laughed in his sleep, and the other cried, 'Murder!', which woke them both. But they said a short prayer together and went back to sleep.

Macbeth thought he heard another voice, which cried, 'Sleep no more! Glamis has murdered sleep, and therefore Cawdor shall sleep no more, Macbeth shall sleep no more.'

Frightened by his own imagination, Macbeth returned to his wife, who was beginning to think he had failed in his purpose and left the deed undone. He came in so disordered a state that she blamed him for his lack of firmness and sent him to wash from his hands the blood which covered them. She herself took his knife and marked the cheeks of the servants with blood to make it seem that they were guilty.

Morning came, and with it the discovery of the murder, which could not be hidden. Macbeth and his lady made a great show of grief, and the proofs against the servants were strong, but everyone still thought Macbeth had done the deed, since his reasons for doing it were so much stronger. Duncan's two sons escaped – Malcolm, the oldest, to the English court, and the youngest, Donalbain, to Ireland.

When the king's sons, who should have worn their father's crown, had left, Macbeth was made king, and so the witches' words came true.

◆

In spite of their success, Macbeth and his queen could not forget the other words of the witches: that although Macbeth would be king, not his children but the children of Banquo would be kings after him. The thought of this troubled them so much that they decided to put to death both Banquo and his son.

They organized a great supper, to which they invited all the chief lords; and, among the rest, Banquo and his son Fleance were respectfully invited. Banquo, arriving at the palace at night, was attacked and killed by murderers hired by Macbeth; but in the fight Fleance escaped.

At supper the queen, whose manners were most friendly and

royal, played the hostess with a gracefulness which pleased everyone present. And Macbeth spoke freely with his lords, saying that every man of honour in the country was under his roof except his good friend Banquo. As he spoke these words, the ghost of Banquo entered the room and placed himself on the chair where Macbeth was about to sit. Though Macbeth was a brave man who could have faced the devil without trembling, his cheeks turned white with fear, and he stood fixed to the floor in shock. His queen and all the lords, who only saw him looking (as they thought) at an empty chair, took this for a moment of craziness. But Macbeth continued to see the ghost, and addressed it with words that sounded crazy but were full of meaning. His queen, fearing that their secret would become public, sent the guests away with great speed, excusing her husband's weakness as a sickness he was often troubled with.

Macbeth's mind was now full of such fears. His queen and he had their sleep broken with terrible dreams. They were troubled both by the blood of Banquo and by the escape of Fleance, whom they now looked on as the father of a line of kings who would keep their own children from the title. They found no peace, and Macbeth decided to find the witches once again, and to learn from them the worst that could happen.

◆

He found them in a cave in a wild part of the country, where they, expecting him, were making their evil spells to call up the spirits of the dead that would show them the future. They mixed parts of animals, birds, snakes and poisonous plants, and the finger of a dead child. All these were boiled up in a large pot, and as the mixture grew too hot it was mixed with monkey's blood. Into this they poured the blood of a pig that had eaten her own young. In this way, they said, they were able to make the spirits of the dead answer their questions.

They asked Macbeth whether he would prefer to have his doubts removed by them or by their masters, the spirits. He, not at all frightened by the ceremonies he saw, answered, 'Where are they? Let me see them.' The first spirit appeared in the form of an armed head, and he called Macbeth by name and told him to be careful of the Lord of Fife; and Macbeth thanked him, because he hated Macduff, the Lord of Fife.

And the second spirit appeared in the likeness of a bloody child, and he called Macbeth by name and told him to have no fear – that no man born of a woman would have the power to hurt him. 'Then live, Macduff!' cried the king. 'Why need I fear you? But I will make quite sure that I am safe. You shall not live; then I can tell pale-hearted Fear that it is lying to me, and I can sleep through the loudest thunder.'

When that spirit had been sent away, a third appeared in the form of a child king, with a tree in his hand. He called Macbeth by name, and comforted him, saying that he would never be beaten until Birnam Wood came to Dunsinane Hill.

'Sweet words! Good!' cried Macbeth. 'Who can unfix the forest, and move it from its roots? I see I shall live for the usual period of a man's life, and not be cut off by a bloody death. But my heart beats to know one thing. Tell me, if your art can tell so much, if Banquo's children shall ever rule in this kingdom?'

The pot sank into the ground, and music was heard, and eight shadows like kings passed by Macbeth; the last of these was Banquo, bearing a glass which showed the figures of many more, and Banquo, all bloody, smiled at Macbeth, and pointed to them. So Macbeth knew that these were the children of Banquo, who would be kings after him in Scotland. The witches, making a show of respect to Macbeth, disappeared. And from this time the thoughts of Macbeth were all bloody and terrible.

The first thing Macbeth heard when he left the witches' cave was that Macduff had escaped to England to join the army which was forming against him under Malcolm, Duncan's eldest son, in the hope of winning back the crown for Malcolm, the lawful king. Macbeth, stung with anger, attacked the castle of Macduff, and killed his wife and children.

These and similar deeds turned the minds of all his chief lords against him. Those that could, went to join Malcolm and Macduff, who were now coming close with a powerful army which they had raised in England. The rest secretly wished them success, though for fear of Macbeth they could take no open part in the fighting.

Everybody hated him and believed him to be a murderer. Macbeth began to wish that he were like Duncan, who slept peacefully in his grave after evil had done its worst. Neither steel nor poison, neither hatred at home nor enemies abroad could hurt him now.

At this time the queen, who had been his only companion in his evil deeds and on whose breast he could sometimes take a short rest from those terrible dreams which interrupted their sleep each night, died; death probably came by her own hand because she was unable to bear her guilt and public hatred. Macbeth was left alone, without a soul to love or care for him, or a friend with whom he could discuss his evil plans.

He grew tired of life, and wished for death; but the arrival of Malcolm's army brought back what remained of his old courage, and he decided to die in battle. Besides this, the hollow promises of the witches had filled him with a false confidence, and he remembered the sayings of the spirits, that no man born of a woman would hurt him, and that he would never be beaten until Birnam Wood came to Dunsinane, which he thought could never happen. So he shut himself up in his strong castle, and waited for the arrival of Malcolm. Then one day a messenger came to him, pale and shaking with fear, almost unable to report what he had seen. He said that as he stood on watch on the hill, he looked towards Birnam, and it seemed that the wood began to move! 'Liar and slave!' cried Macbeth. 'If you are lying, you will hang alive from a tree until hunger ends your life. If your story is true, I do not care if you do the same with me.' Macbeth now began to lose his strength of purpose, and to doubt the words of the spirits. He was not to fear until Birnam Wood came to Dunsinane – and now a wood was moving!

'But,' he said, 'if what he states is true, let us arm ourselves and go out. We will not run away, nor stay here; I am beginning to be tired of the sun, and wish my life were at an end.' With these hopeless words he marched towards his enemies, who had now come up close to the castle.

◆

The moving wood is easily explained. When the attacking army marched through Birnam Wood, Malcolm, as a skilful general, commanded each of his soldiers to cut down a branch and carry it in front of him to hide the true numbers of his army. This had at a distance given the appearance which had frightened the messenger. So the words of the spirit came true, in a sense different from that in which Macbeth had understood them, and his confidence began to disappear.

And now a terrible battle took place, in which Macbeth, though poorly helped by those who called themselves his friends, fought with extreme anger and courage, cutting to pieces all who were opposed to him, until he came to where Macduff was fighting. Remembering that the spirit had warned him not to quarrel with Macduff in particular, he would have turned. But Macduff, who had been hunting him during the whole battle, prevented him from leaving, and a violent fight followed. Macbeth, whose soul was marked with the blood of that family already, wanted to refuse the fight. But Macduff, remembering his dead wife and children, called him an evil murderer and forced him to defend himself.

Then Macbeth remembered the words of the spirit; and, smiling confidently, he said to Macduff, 'You are wasting your time, Macduff. You can hurt the air with your sword, as easily as you can hurt me. I have a magic life, which cannot be taken by a man born of a woman.'

'Put no hope in your magic,' said Macduff, 'and let that lying spirit whom you have served tell you that Macduff was never born of a woman, not in the usual way in which men are born, but was taken from his mother before the time.'

The trembling Macbeth felt his last hope disappear. 'Do not in future let people believe the lies of witches and spirits, who deceive us with words which have double senses,' he cried. 'I will not fight with you.'

'Then live!' said Macduff. 'We will show you, as men show monsters, with a painted board, on which will be written "Here men may see the cruel Macbeth!"'

'Never,' said Macbeth, whose courage returned with lack of hope. 'I will not live to kiss the ground before young Malcolm's feet, and to be shamed by the shouts of the crowd. Though Birnam Wood has come to Dunsinane, and you are a man who was never born of a woman, I will make one last attempt.' With these words he threw himself on Macduff, who, after a violent struggle, beat him in the end. Macduff cut off Macbeth's head and made a present of it to the young and lawful king, Malcolm, who took back the kingdom which he had so long been without, to the joyful cries of the lords and the people.

Twelfth Night, or What You Will

CHARACTERS

Orsino, Duke of Illyria

Sebastian, a young man of Messaline

Antonio, a sea captain and friend of Sebastian

Another sea captain

Servants

A priest

Viola, twin sister of Sebastian, who dresses herself as the servant, *Cesario*

Olivia

Sebastian and his sister Viola, a young gentleman and lady of Messaline, were twins, and from their birth they were so similar in appearance that, except for the difference in their dress, they could not be told apart. They were both born in the same hour, and in another hour they were both in danger of death, for they were shipwrecked on the coast of Illyria as they were making a journey together. The ship which they were on hit a rock in a great storm, and a very small number of the people on board escaped with their lives. The captain of the ship, with a few of the sailors who were saved, reached land in a small boat, and with them they brought Viola safely to shore. But she, poor lady, instead of being grateful for her own safety, began to cry for the loss of her brother. The captain comforted her by telling her that he had seen her brother, when the ship was sinking, tie himself to a strong pole, on which he was carried up above the waves. Viola was much comforted by the hope this account gave her, and now considered how she was to live in a strange country so far from home; and she asked the captain if he knew anything of Illyria.

'Yes, very well, madam,' replied the captain, 'since I was born less than three hours' travel from this place.'

'Who governs here?' said Viola. The captain told her that Illyria was governed by Orsino, a duke who was kind and wise. Viola said she had heard her father speak of Orsino, and that he was then unmarried.

'And he still is,' said the captain; 'or was so very recently. Only a month ago, when I was here, people were saying that Orsino loved fair Olivia, the daughter of a lord who died 12 months ago and left Olivia to the care of her brother, who also died. And for the love of this dear brother, they say, she has hidden herself from the sight and company of men.'

Viola, who was herself very unhappy about the loss of her brother, wished she could live with this lady who cried for the death of her own brother. She asked the captain if he could take her to Olivia, saying she would gladly serve this lady. But he replied that this would be a hard thing to do, because the Lady Olivia would let no person into her house since her brother's death, not even the duke himself. Then Viola formed another plan in her mind, which was to dress as a man and to serve the Duke Orsino as a servant. It was a strange idea for a young lady to put on men's clothes and pretend to be a boy; but she was young, beautiful, alone and in a foreign land, and this was her excuse.

She had noticed that the captain showed a friendly concern for her, so she trusted him with her plan, and he gladly promised to help her. Viola gave him money, and told him to get her clothes of the same colour and in the same fashion as her brother Sebastian used to wear. And when she was dressed in her manly clothes, she looked so exactly like her brother that they were in fact mistaken for each other; for, as we shall soon discover, Sebastian was also saved.

When he had turned this pretty lady into a gentleman, Viola's good friend, the captain, who had some power at court, got her presented to Orsino under the name of Cesario. The duke was pleased with the appearance and speech of this good-looking young man, and made Cesario one of his servants, as Viola wished. She carried out the duties of her new post so well, and showed such obedience and love for her lord, that she soon became his favourite attendant. To Cesario, Orsino told the whole history of his love for the lady Olivia; how she, uninterested in the services he did for her, and disliking his person, refused to admit him to her presence. And for the love of this lady who had treated him so unkindly, Orsino had stopped enjoying sports and other manly activities, and spent his time in dishonourable laziness, listening to soft music and gentle love songs; and leaving the company of his wise and learned lords, he now talked all day to young Cesario.

It is a dangerous thing for young women to be the friends of good-looking young dukes, which Viola soon found to her sorrow. In spite of all that Orsino told her he suffered for Olivia, she realized that she herself was suffering for the love of him; and she often wondered how Olivia could care so little for this lord and master, whom she thought no one could look at without the deepest admiration. So she said gently to Orsino that it was a pity he should desire a lady who was so blind to his true worth, adding, 'If a lady were to love you, my lord, as you love Olivia (and perhaps there may be one who does), and if you could not love her in return, would you not tell her that you could not love, and must she not be satisfied with this answer?'

But Orsino would not listen to this reasoning, saying that it was impossible for any woman to love as he did. He said that no woman's heart was big enough to hold so much love, and therefore it was unfair to compare the love of any lady for him to his love for Olivia. Viola had the greatest respect for the duke's opinions, but she could not help thinking this was not quite true, since she thought her heart had quite as much love in it as Orsino's had; and she said, 'Ah, but I know, my lord.'

'What do you know, Cesario?' said Orsino.

'I know very well,' replied Viola, 'how much women may love men. Their hearts are true as ours are. My father had a daughter who loved a man, as I would perhaps love you, if I were a woman.'

'And what is her history?' said Orsino.

'An empty page, my lord,' replied Viola. 'She never told anyone of her love, but let her secret, like a worm in an unopened flower, feed on her rosy cheek. She grew sick in thought, and sat like Patience in a picture, smiling at Grief.'

◆

While they were talking, a gentleman entered whom the duke had sent to Olivia, and said, 'My lord, I was not admitted into the presence of the lady, but she sent this message: "Until seven years have passed, the sky itself shall not see my face; until then I will walk with my face covered, watering my room with my tears for the sad memory of my dead brother." '

On hearing this, the duke cried, 'Oh, if she has a heart like this, to pay this debt of love to a dead brother, how deeply she will love a husband!'

And then he said to Viola, 'You know, Cesario, I have told you all the secrets of my heart; therefore, good youth, go to Olivia's house. Make them let you in; stand at her doors, and tell her that you will not move until you speak to her.'

'And if I do speak to her, my lord, what then?' said Viola.

'Oh, then,' replied Orsino, 'unfold to her the depth of my love. Tell her how I honour her. You are the right person to act out my grief; she will pay more attention to you than to someone of more serious looks.'

Away then went Viola; but she did not go gladly, since her job was to ask a lady to become the wife of the man she wished to marry. But having promised, she carried it out; and Olivia soon heard that a youth was at her door asking to speak to her.

'I told him,' said the servant, 'that you were sick. He said he knew you were, and that was why he came to speak with you. I told him that you were asleep, and he continued to say that he must speak with you. What shall I say to him, lady? For he seems determined to speak with you whether you want to or not.'

Olivia, interested to see who this urgent messenger might be, said he could come in and, covering her face, she said she would hear Orsino's messages once more.

As she entered, Viola put on her most manly air and, using the fine language of great men's messengers, said to the lady, 'Most lovely and unequalled beauty, I pray you tell me if you are the lady of the house; for I would be sorry to waste my speech on someone else, since it is very well written and I have gone to great trouble to learn it.'

'Where do you come from, sir?' said Olivia.

'I can say little more than I have studied,' replied Viola, 'and that question is outside my part.'

'Are you an actor?' said Olivia.

'No,' replied Viola, 'but I am not that which I play.' (She meant that she, being a woman, was pretending to be a man.) And again she asked Olivia if she were the lady of the house. Olivia said she was; and then Viola, having more desire to see her face than to deliver her master's message, said, 'Good lady, let me see your face.'

Olivia was happy to do so; for this proud beauty, whom the duke Orsino had loved for so long, had fallen in love at first sight with the messenger (as she thought him), the young Cesario.

◆

When Viola asked to see her face, Olivia said, 'Have you been commanded by your lord and master to do business with my face?' And then, forgetting her decision to cover her face for seven long years, she uncovered it, saying, 'But I will draw the curtain and show the picture. Is it not well done?'

Viola replied, 'It is beauty truly mixed; the red and white on your cheeks have been painted on by Nature's own hand. You are the most cruel lady alive, if you take these beauties to the grave and leave the world no copy.'

'Oh, sir,' replied Olivia, 'I will not be so cruel. The world may have a list of them: two lips, just red enough; two grey eyes, with lids; one neck; one chin; and so on. Were you sent here to praise me?'

Viola replied, 'I see what you are: you are too proud, but you are fair. My lord and master loves you dearly.'

'Your lord,' said Olivia, 'knows my mind. I cannot love him, although I have no doubt he is a good man; I know him to be of high birth, of fresh and spotless youth. Everyone says that he is wise, polite, and brave, but I cannot love him and he should have accepted that answer long ago.'

'If I loved you as my master does,' said Viola, 'I would build a wooden hut at your gates, and call your name. I would write poems about Olivia, and sing them in the dead of night; your name would sound among the hills, and I would make the spirit of the air cry out "Olivia". Oh, you would not rest between earth and air, but you would pity me.'

'There is much that you can do,' said Olivia. 'What is your birth?'

Viola replied, 'Higher than my fortunes. I am a gentleman.'

Olivia now sent Viola away, saying, 'Go to your master, and tell him I cannot love him. Let him send no more messages, unless perhaps you come again to tell me how he takes the news.'

And Viola left, saying goodbye to the lady by the name of Fair Cruelty. When she had gone, Olivia repeated the words: 'Higher than my fortunes. I am a gentleman.' And she said out loud, 'I will swear he is; his tongue, his face, his appearance, action, and spirit plainly show he is a gentleman.' And then she wished Cesario was the duke; and realizing how firm his hold on her heart had become, she blamed herself for her sudden love. But the gentle blame which people lay on their own faults has no deep root. And soon the Lady Olivia forgot the difference between her own fortunes and those of this messenger, as well as the shame which is the chief beauty of a lady's character. So she decided to try to gain the love of young Cesario. She sent a servant after him with a diamond ring, saying that he had left it with her as a present from Orsino. She hoped, by making Cesario a present of the ring, that she would give him some knowledge of her plan. And truly it did make Viola think; knowing that Orsino had sent no ring, she began to remember that Olivia's looks and manner were full of admiration, and she soon guessed that her master's loved one had fallen in love with her. 'Oh, dear,' said she, 'the poor lady might as well love a dream. My clothes have caused terrible problems. Now Olivia loves me as I do Orsino.'

Viola returned to Orsino's palace and told her lord of her lack of success, repeating Olivia's command that the duke should trouble her no more. But still the duke went on hoping that the gentle Cesario would in time be able to persuade her to show some pity, and therefore he told him to go to her again the next day.

◆

When Viola made her second visit to Olivia, she found no difficulty in entering. Servants soon discover when their ladies are pleased to talk with good-looking young messengers; and the moment Viola arrived, the gates were thrown wide open, and Cesario was shown into Olivia's presence with great respect. And when Viola told Olivia that she had come once more to speak for her lord, this lady said, 'I asked you never to speak of him again; but if you would like to speak of something else, I would rather hear you speak than hear music from heaven.'

This was plain speaking, but Olivia soon explained herself still more plainly, and openly admitted her love. Viola hurried from her presence, saying she would never again come to speak of Orsino's love; and the only reply she gave to Olivia was that she would never love any woman.

No sooner had Viola left the lady than she found herself in trouble. A gentleman, who had been refused by Olivia and had now learned that that lady had fallen in love with Cesario, called on the messenger to fight with him. What should poor Viola do? Although she had a man's appearance, she had a true woman's heart and was afraid to look at her own sword.

When she saw him coming towards her with his sword out, she began to think of saying that she was a woman. But she was saved immediately from her terror, and the shame of such a discovery, by a stranger who was passing by; as if he were her oldest and dearest friend, he said to her opponent, 'If this young gentleman has done you wrong, I will take responsibility for his fault; and if you offend him, I will fight you.'

Before Viola had time to thank him, officers of justice came up and seized the stranger in the duke's name to answer for an offence he had been guilty of some years before, and he said to Viola, 'This comes from searching for you.' Then he asked her for a bag of money, saying, 'Now my situation makes me ask for my money back, and what I cannot do for you saddens me much more than what is happening to myself. You are surprised, but do not worry.'

His words really surprised Viola, and she told him she did not know him, nor had she ever received money from him; but for the kindness he had just shown her, she offered him a small sum of money, almost everything she possessed. And now the stranger spoke cruelly, saying she was ungrateful and unkind. He said to the officers, 'I saved this young man, whom you see here, from the jaws of death, and for him alone I came to Illyria and have fallen into this danger.' But the officers cared little about the complaints of their prisoner, and they hurried him off, saying, 'What is that to us?' And as he was carried away, he called Viola 'Sebastian' and 'ungrateful' as long as he was within hearing. When Viola heard herself called Sebastian, she realized she had been mistaken for her brother, and she began to hope that it was her brother whose life this man had saved. And so it was.

◆

The stranger, whose name was Antonio, was a sea captain. He had taken Sebastian up into his ship, when, almost dead with tiredness, he was floating on the pole to which he had tied himself in the storm.

Antonio and Sebastian had landed together only a few hours before Antonio met Viola. He had given his money to Sebastian, telling him to use it freely if he saw anything he wished to buy, and telling him he would wait while Sebastian went to see the town. But when Sebastian did not return at the agreed time, Antonio had gone out to look for him. So, since Viola was dressed the same, and looked so much like her brother, Antonio had drawn his sword (as he thought) in defence of the young man he had saved; and when Sebastian (as he supposed) would not admit to knowing him or give him his own money, no wonder he told him he was ungrateful.

When Antonio had gone, Viola, fearing a second invitation to fight, ran home as fast as she could. She had not been gone long when her enemy thought he saw her return, but it was her brother Sebastian who happened to arrive at this place. The unhappy rival said, 'Now, sir, have I met with you again? There, for you,' and struck him. Sebastian returned the blow, and pulled out his sword.

A lady now put a stop to this fight, for Olivia came out of the house and she, also mistaking Sebastian for Cesario, asked him to come into her house, saying she was very sorry that he had been attacked so rudely. Though Sebastian was as surprised at the kindness of this lady as at the rudeness of his unknown enemy, he was glad to go in, and Olivia was pleased to find that Cesario (as she thought) had become more friendly.

◆

Sebastian did not object at all to the kindness the lady showed him, but he wondered what the reason for it was, and he rather thought Olivia was not in her right senses. But seeing that she owned a fine house, and that she managed her affairs and seemed to govern her home wisely, and that in everything except her sudden love for him she appeared to be in full possession of her reason, he allowed her to be kind to him. When Olivia found Cesario in this good humour, and fearing he might change his mind, she proposed that, as she had a priest in the house, they should be married at once. Sebastian agreed; and when the marriage ceremony was over, he left his lady for a short time, intending to go and tell his friend Antonio about his good fortune.

While this was happening, Orsino came to visit Olivia; and as he arrived in front of Olivia's house, the officers of justice brought the prisoner, Antonio, in front of the duke. Viola was with Orsino; and when Antonio saw Viola, whom he still imagined to be Sebastian, he told the duke how he had saved this youth from the dangers of the sea.

But now the Lady Olivia came out from her house, so the

duke could no longer attend to Antonio's story, and he said, 'Here comes my love: now heaven walks on earth! But you, sir, I do not understand. It is now three months since this youth first attended on me.' Then he ordered Antonio to be taken to one side. But Orsino's heavenly love soon gave the duke cause to complain as much as Antonio had done about the ungrateful Cesario, for all the words he could hear Olivia speak were words of kindness to Cesario. And when he found his servant had obtained this place in Olivia's heart, he promised to punish him; and as he was leaving, he called Viola to follow him. Though his anger was so great it seemed he was going to put Viola to death immediately, her love made her strong and brave, and she said she would most joyfully suffer death if her master wished it.

But Olivia was not prepared to lose her husband, and she cried, 'Where is my Cesario going?' Viola replied, 'After him whom I love more than my life.' Olivia cried out loudly that Cesario was her husband, and sent for the priest, who declared that less than two hours had passed since he had married the lady Olivia to this young man. Viola cried that she was not married to Olivia, but Orsino would not listen; the statements of Olivia and the priest made Orsino believe that this young man had robbed him of the love he prized above his own life.

But then a strange thing happened! Another Cesario entered, and addressed Olivia as his wife. This new Cesario was Sebastian, the real husband of Olivia; and when their wonder at seeing two persons with the same face, the same voice, and the same dress had passed, the brother and sister began to question each other. Viola could hardly be persuaded that her brother was living, and Sebastian did not know why the sister whom he thought had drowned was dressed like a young man. But Viola said that she really was Viola, and his sister.

When everything was understood, they laughed at Olivia for falling in love with a woman; and Olivia was not at all unhappy when she found she had married the brother instead of the sister.

The hopes of Orsino had been ended for ever by this marriage of Olivia, and with his hopes all his love seemed to disappear, and all his thoughts were fixed on his favourite, young Cesario. He looked at Viola with great attention, and he remembered how very beautiful he had always thought Cesario was. And then he remembered how often she had said she loved him, which at the time seemed only the dutiful words of a good servant; but now he guessed that something more had been meant. For many of her pretty sayings, which had appeared at the time to have double meanings, came now into his mind, and he decided to try to make Viola his wife. And he said to her (he still could not help calling her 'Cesario' and 'boy'), 'Boy, you have told me a thousand times that you could never love a woman, and for your good service to me you shall now be your master's wife.'

Olivia, seeing that the love which she had refused now belonged to Viola, invited them to enter her house, and offered the help of the good priest who had married her to Sebastian that morning. So the twin brother and sister were both married on the same day, and the storm and shipwreck which had separated them were the cause of their good fortune. Viola was now the wife of Orsino, the Duke of Illyria, and Sebastian the husband of the rich and beautiful Lady Olivia.

ACTIVITIES

The Tempest

Before you read

1 Read the Introduction to this book and answer these questions.
   a In which order did Shakespeare write the seven plays from which the stories in this book are taken?
   b Which of these stories was written by Charles Lamb?
2 Look at the Word List at the back of the book. Find words for
   a people
   b creatures, magical or real
3 This is a story about a man and his daughter who have lived alone on an island for many years. If you had to live alone for a long time on an island, what three things would you like to have with you?

While you read

4 Are these sentences true (✓) or false (✗)?
   a Ariel is a witch's son.   .....
   b Only one person can see Ariel.   .....
   c Prospero can control the weather.   .....
   d Prospero loves books.   .....
   e Prospero sinks his enemies' ship.   .....
   f Miranda displeases her father with her disobedience.   .....
   g Antonio recognizes his brother immediately.   .....
   h Prospero forgives his enemies.   .....
   i Miranda will become the Queen of Naples when
     she marries Ferdinand.   .....
   j Ariel returns to Naples with Prospero and Miranda.   .....

After you read

5 How do these people or creatures feel about each other? Why?
   a Ariel and Caliban   d Prospero and Ferdinand
   b Prospero and Antonio   e The King of Naples and Miranda
   c Prospero and Ariel

6 Who might have these thoughts, and about what or whom? Why?

    a 'You are my prisoners.'

    b 'Why did I fall over?'

    c 'You can have it – I don't want it.'

    d 'I would have been unhappy if you hadn't been with me.'

    e 'Get the evil witch away from here!'

    f 'I can't let this develop too quickly.'

    g 'My plan's going to succeed.'

    h 'We were wrong to do that.'

    i 'What's that wild music?'

7 Answer these questions.

    a Which of her father's magic powers does Miranda not know about?

    b Why do Ariel and Prospero have an argument?

    c Why does Ferdinand take out his sword?

    d Who is filled with 'grief and terror'? Why?

    e When do Antonio and the King of Naples realize who Prospero is?

    f What is the weather like on the journey back to Italy? Why?

A Midsummer Night's Dream

Before you read

8 In this story, fathers are allowed by law to choose husbands for their daughters. Do arranged marriages like this exist in your country? What are the advantages and disadvantages of arranged marriages? Are they generally a good idea, in your opinion? Why (not)?

While you read

9 Who are these sentences about?

    a He has chosen a husband for his daughter.   ....

    b Hermia loves him.   ....

    c Helena loves him.   ....

    d He enjoys playing tricks.   ....

    e Oberon feels sorry for her.   ....

f Lysander and Demetrius fall in love with her
because of love-juice in their eyes.   ....

g She falls in love with a man with an ass's head. ....

h He still has love-juice in his eyes at the end
of the story.   ....

After you read

10 What problems do these people have with each other? How are
they solved?

    a Egeus and Hermia   **c** Lysander and Hermia

    b Helena and Demetrius   **d** Oberon and Titania

11 Work with another student. Have this conversation.

    Student A: You are Egeus. You want Hermia to marry Demetrius
and not Lysander. Tell her why.

    Student B: You are Hermia. You do not want to marry Demetrius.
Tell your father why.

12 Is Egeus a bad father? Why (not)? Discuss your ideas with another
student.

Much Ado About Nothing

Before you read

13 In this story, two people who dislike each other suddenly begin to
love each other. Why might this happen? How likely is this in real
life?

While you read

14 Circle the correct answer.

    a Hero and Beatrice are *sisters / cousins / friends*.

    b Beatrice thinks that Benedick is a *coward / liar / joker*.

    c *Benedick / Claudio / Pedro* loves Hero.

    d Benedick hears *two / three / four* men talking about him and
Beatrice.

    e Beatrice hears Hero talking to *Claudio / Ursula / Margaret*.

    f Claudio and Pedro see *Hero / Beatrice / Margaret* talking from a
window, but they think it is *Hero / Beatrice / Margaret*.

g During the wedding, Hero's honour is defended by *Leonato / Claudio / the priest*.

h Beatrice wants Benedick to kill *Borachio / Claudio / John*.

i Claudio and Pedro *are ordered / decide / refuse* to fight Leonato.

j Benedick and Beatrice *announce / deny / joke about* their love for each other.

After you read

15 What problems do these people have with each other? How are they solved?

   a Benedick and Beatrice

   b Claudio and Hero

   c Pedro and John

16 Work with another student. Have this conversation between Leonato and Pedro.

   Student A: You are Pedro. You think that John is a bad man. Tell Leonato why you do not want him to come to Messina.

   Student B: You are Leonato. You think that Pedro is wrong about John. Tell him why.

17 Work in pairs and discuss these questions.

   a 'The trouble at the wedding was Claudio's fault, not John's.' Do you agree with this statement? Why (not)?

   b Will Benedick and Beatrice be happy together? Why (not)?

As You Like It

Before you read

18 In this story, a woman wears a man's clothes and persuades people that she is a man. How easy do you think that it would be to do this in real life?

While you read

19 When do these happen? Number them 1–10.

    a Orlando meets the true duke. .....

    b Orlando saves his brother's life. .....

    c Orlando and Adam arrive in the forest. .....

    d Rosalind dresses like a young man. .....

    e There is a double wedding. .....

    f Duke Frederick sends Rosalind away. .....

    g Orlando meets Rosalind but does not recognize her. .....

    h Rosalind meets Orlando before the wrestling match. .....

    i Celia falls in love with Orlando's brother. .....

    j Rosalind and Celia buy a house in the forest. .....

After you read

20 There are eight mistakes in this short description of the story. Underline them and write a correct description.

Orlando enters a wrestling competition because he wants to be famous. The Duke Frederick is angry because he wins the fight, but Rosalind, the Duke's niece, falls in love with him. She dresses like a young man and runs away to the forest of Arden with Celia, who pretends to be her lover. A few days later, Orlando runs away to the same forest with his faithful servant, Adam. He meets a shepherd, who gives them food and shelter. Rosalind, who is still dressed like man, meets Orlando, who has been singing love songs for her. He recognizes her and agrees to visit her regularly. Later, he is wounded while trying to kill his cruel brother, Oliver. In the end, Celia marries Oliver; Rosalind marries Orlando; the Duke Frederick dies and the true duke returns to his palace.

21 Work with another student. Have this conversation.

    Student A: You are the Duke Frederick. Tell the religious man why you have come to the forest of Arden.

    Student B: You are the religious man. Persuade Frederick to change his mind and give his stolen property back to his brother.

The Merchant of Venice

Before you read

22 'It is impossible to succeed in life without borrowing money.' Do you agree with this statement? Why (not)? Discuss your ideas with another student.

While you read

23 Are these sentences about Shylock (S), Bassanio (B) or Antonio (A)?

    a He makes a big profit on the money that he lends. .....

    b He spends too much money. .....

    c He borrows three thousand pounds. .....

    d He plans a secret revenge. .....

    e Portia loves him. .....

    f He loses his ships. .....

    g His offer of money is refused. .....

    h He does not recognize Portia. .....

    i The duke saves his life. .....

    j Portia is angry with him. .....

After you read

24 Who is speaking, and to whom? What are they talking about?

    a 'Does a dog have money?'

    b 'I will sign this paper.'

    c 'This house, these servants and myself are yours.'

    d 'Madam, it is true, if you approve it.'

    e 'Oh, wise young judge, how I honour you!'

    f 'Be merciful; take the money.'

    g 'You must prepare your breast for the knife.'

    h 'It does not say so in the contract.'

    i 'Get down on your knees and ask him to pardon you.'

    j 'I am the unhappy cause of these quarrels'.

25 Discuss these questions with another student.

    a Do you feel sorry for Shylock? Why (not)?

    b What lessons can we learn from this story?

Macbeth

Before you read

26 Is it possible to see into the future? Would you like to know *your* future? Why (not)?

While you read

27 Write the missing words.

    a The third .... says that Macbeth will become king.

    b .... warns Macbeth not to listen to the witches.

    c Lady Macbeth cannot kill the .... because he reminds her of her father.

    d During the great supper, Macbeth sees Banquo's ....

    e The witches tell Macbeth that he is safe unless Birnam .... comes to Dunsinane Hill.

    f Macbeth kills ....'s wife and children.

    g Lady Macbeth kills ....

    h Macbeth decides to die in ....

    i .... kills Macbeth.

    j .... becomes king after Macbeth's death.

After you read

28 How do these people feel about Macbeth? Why?

    a Banquo   **d** Macduff

    b Lady Macbeth   **e** Malcolm and Donalbain

    c Duncan   **f** Fleance

29 Work with another student. Have this conversation.

    Student A: You are Macbeth. You do not want to kill Duncan. Tell your wife why.

    Student B: You are Lady Macbeth. You think that your husband is a coward. Tell him why he must kill Duncan.

30 Who is most to blame for Macbeth's evil actions – the witches, Lady Macbeth or Macbeth himself? Why? Discuss your ideas with another student.

Twelfth Night, or What You Will

Before you read

31 This story involves twins who look exactly the same as each other. What amusing situations can you imagine them in?

While you read

32 Do these sentences describe Viola (V), Olivia (O) or both (B)?

   a She is sad about her brother.   .....

   b She sees no visitors.   .....

   c She dresses as a man.   .....

   d She loves Orsino.   .....

   e She loves Cesario.   .....

   f She is given a ring.   .....

   g She saves Sebastian from a fight.   .....

   h Orsino is angry with her.   .....

   i She marries Orsino.   .....

After you read

33 What problems do these people have with each other? How are their problems solved?

   a Viola and Sebastian   **d** Viola and Olivia

   b Orsino and Olivia   **e** Viola and Antonio

   c Viola and Orsino

34 Work with another student. Have this conversation.

   Student A: You are Orsino. You are angry with Viola for deceiving you and winning Olivia's love. Tell her why she must be punished.

   Student B: You are Viola. Explain why you deceived Orsino and why you do not deserve to be punished.

Writing

35 (*The Tempest*) What happens to the King of Naples and Antonio from the time of the shipwreck to their meeting with Prospero?

36 (*A Midsummer Night's Dream*) Write about the importance of love-juice in the story. What problems does it cause and solve?

37 (*Much Ado About Nothing*) You are Beatrice. Write a letter to a friend describing your confused feelings towards Benedick.

38 (*As You Like It*) You are Orlando. Write a letter to a friend describing your confused feelings towards Ganymede.

39 (*The Merchant of Venice*) You are a reporter. Write about the courtroom scene for your newspaper.

40 (*Macbeth*) Imagine that Macbeth does not die at the end of the story but is taken prisoner. You are Macbeth's lawyer. You think that Macbeth should be forgiven for his crimes. Write your speech.

41 (*Macbeth*) How is *Macbeth* different from the other stories in this book? Which type of story do you prefer? Why?

42 (*Twelfth Night*) What happens to Sebastian from the time of the shipwreck to his meeting with Viola? Write his story.

43 Choose one of these and explain how they are important in these stories: shipwrecks; women dressed as men; magic.

44 In these stories, many people are forgiven for their crimes. Who are they, what are their crimes and why are they forgiven? Do they deserve to be forgiven? Why (not)?

WORD LIST

ado (n) time-wasting activity

approve (v) to believe that someone or something is acceptable; to agree to something

ass (n) a grey or brown animal like a small horse with long ears

attendant (n) someone who goes with another person to help or protect them

comedy (n) an amusing play; a play with a happy ending

companion (n) someone who you spend a lot of time with

deed (n) an action

duke (n) a man with the highest social position below a prince

crown (n/v) a circle of gold and jewels worn by kings and queens on their heads; when somebody is crowned, that person becomes a king or queen

fairy (n) an imaginary creature with magic powers that looks like a very small person with wings

grief (n) a feeling of extreme sadness, especially after someone has died

influence (v) to affect the way that someone behaves or thinks

jester (n) a male entertainer who is paid to tell jokes and stories

kingdom (n) a country that has a king or a queen

lamb (n) a young sheep

merchant (n) someone who buys and sells large quantities of goods

mercy (n) kindness and a willingness to forgive

monster (n) a large, ugly, frightening creature

obedience (n) the act of obeying a person, law or rule

opponent (n) someone who you try to defeat in a competition

rank (n) a person's level of importance in society

shepherd (n) someone who takes care of sheep

spell (n) a piece of magic, or the words that make the magic happen

tale (n) a story about imaginary or exciting events

tempest (n) a violent storm

tremble (v) to shake because you are worried, afraid or excited

witch (n) a woman who is believed to have magic powers, especially to do bad things

worm (n) a small creature with a long, soft body and no legs that lives in the ground

worthy (adj) good enough to deserve respect, admiration or attention

wrestle (v) to fight by holding someone and trying to push them to the ground

More Tales from Shakespeare
Charles and Mary Lamb

This collection of six short stories, based on Shakespeare's plays, is the perfect introduction to one of the world's greatest writers. Meet the tragic young lovers Romeo and Juliet, mad King Lear, angry young Hamlet, and many more of the most famous characters in world literature.

Jane Eyre
Charlotte Brontë

Jane Eyre, a poor orphan, grows up in misery until she becomes the governess in the house of wealthy Mr Rochester and falls in love. But mysterious events take place in the house at night, and Mr Rochester appears to be hiding a terrible secret. Can Jane even hope for happiness?

Pride and Prejudice
Jane Austen

Jane and Elizabeth Bennet are the oldest of five sisters in need of husbands, but it isn't easy to find the right man. Are Mr Bingley, Mr Darcy and Mr Wickham all that they seem? Will pride and prejudice ever be defeated in the search for true love?

There are hundreds of Penguin Readers to choose from – world classics, film adaptations, modern-day crime and adventure, short stories, biographies, American classics, non-fiction, plays ...

For a complete list of all Penguin Readers titles, please contact your local Pearson Longman office or visit our website.

www.penguinreaders.com

The War of the Worlds
H.G. Wells

The War of the Worlds is one of the most frightening science fiction novels ever written. When a spaceship falls from the sky and lands in southern England, few people are worried. But when strange creatures climb out and start killing, nobody is safe.

The Phantom of the Opera
Gaston Leroux

There is a climate of secrecy and fear at the Paris Opera. People are dying and a beautiful, talented young singer has disappeared. Is this the work of the Opera ghost? Is the ghost a man or a monster? And what else will he do to get what he wants?

Rebecca
Daphne du Maurier

After the death of his beautiful wife, Rebecca, Maxim de Winter goes to Monte Carlo to forget the past. There he marries a quiet young woman and takes her back to Manderley, his lovely country home. But the memory of Rebecca casts a dark shadow on the new marriage. Then the discovery of a sunken boat shatters the new Mrs de Winter's dream of a happy life.

There are hundreds of Penguin Readers to choose from – world classics, film adaptations, modern-day crime and adventure, short stories, biographies, American classics, non-fiction, plays ...

For a complete list of all Penguin Readers titles, please contact your local Pearson Longman office or visit our website.

Longman Dictionaries

Express yourself with confidence!

Longman has led the way in ELT dictionaries since 1935. We constantly talk to students and teachers around the world to find out what they need from a learner's dictionary.

Why choose a Longman dictionary?

Easy to understand

Longman invented the Defining Vocabulary – 2000 of the most common words which are used to write the definitions in our dictionaries. So Longman definitions are always clear and easy to understand.

Real, natural English

All Longman dictionaries contain natural examples taken from real-life that help explain the meaning of a word and show you how to use it in context.

Avoid common mistakes

Longman dictionaries are written specially for learners, and we make sure that you get all the help you need to avoid common mistakes. We analyse typical learners' mistakes and include notes on how to avoid them.

Innovative CD-ROMs

Longman are leaders in dictionary CD-ROM innovation. Did you know that a dictionary CD-ROM includes features to help improve your pronunciation, help you practice for exams and improve your writing skills?

For details of all Longman dictionaries, and to choose the one that's right for you, visit our website:

www.longman.com/dictionaries